Engine Out

SURVIVAL TACTICS

FIGHTER PILOT TACTICS FOR GENERAL AVIATION
ENGINE LOSS EMERGENCIES

NATE S. "BUSTER" JAROS

First Printing 2016

ISBN 978-1-48359-455-2

Disclaimer:

This book is not meant as a substitute for the individual judgment of the pilot in command. There is no one guide or answer to any given engine out scenario. Remember, you are the pilot in command.

Fly Safe!

TABLE OF CONTENTS

LIST OF ILLUSTRATIONS

ABOUT THE AUTHOR

Nate "Buster" Jaros is a retired USAF fighter pilot with over 2,000 hours in F-16 C/D/CM and T-38A/C aircraft and over 500 hours in General Aviation aircraft. He is currently a Test Pilot and Instructor Pilot with a Major Defense Contractor. He has a Bachelor of Science degree as well as a Master of Business Administration and owns, operates, and maintains a 1969 V-tail Bonanza. Buster currently resides in Las Vegas, Nevada and is a long-time member of the Aircraft Owners and Pilots Association as well as the American Bonanza Society. You can view his webpage at: http://engineout.weebly.com

FOREWORD

Think back to the training you had on engine failures. You were probably flying along at cruise speed at altitude when your instructor reached up, pulled the throttle to idle and announced "you have an engine failure." Your objective was to establish Best Glide speed, pick a field or other emergency landing site, and maneuver the airplane to be in a position to land at your selected spot. When you got within 500 feet of the ground you executed a go-around. If you had a particularly enthusiastic instructor he or she may have pulled the throttle to idle while you were on downwind in the traffic pattern, and you glided to a landing on the runway.

On your Practical Test ("checkride") the examiner was required only to ensure you:

1. Exhibit satisfactory knowledge of the elements related to emergency approach and landing procedures.
2. Analyze the situation and select an appropriate course of action.

3. Establish and maintain the recommended best-glide airspeed, ±10 knots.
4. Select a suitable landing area.
5. Plan and follow a flight pattern to the selected landing area considering altitude, wind, terrain and obstructions.
6. Prepare for landing or go-around as specified by the examiner.
7. Follow the appropriate checklist.

From the FAA Practical Test Standards, Private Pilot – Airplane Single Engine

The FAA provides virtually no guidance on landing site selection, glidepath management, or the transition from glide to landing without power or speed to flare and touch-down. Item 7 on the Practical Test Standards (PTS) checklist perhaps suggests the pilot candidate attempts to troubleshoot and possibly restart the engine, but it does not overtly require it; the follow-on task, Systems and Equipment Malfunctions, includes "partial or complete power loss", "engine roughness or overheat", "carburetor or induction icing", "loss oil pressure" and "fuel starvation" on a list of 14 simulated emergencies on which a candidate may be evaluated, but the examiner need only evaluate three of the 14.

Sure, a flight instructor needs to prepare the pilot candidate to handle any of these items. But the reality is that there often is not a lot of emphasis on anything other than the "dead engine, glide to a field" approach in General Aviation flight instruction and evaluation.

Does this alone really prepare pilots to survive engine failures in single-engine airplanes?

Nate Jaros, a U.S. Air Force fighter pilot and avid general aviation pilot, doesn't think so. He observes that "engine loss training, as well as the level of understanding for a majority of [General Aviation] pilots and CFIs, is severely lacking." Surprised with this realization upon leaving the Air Force and entering the world of personal aviation, Jaros struck out to create "a fighter pilot's view of engine-out training" among General Aviation pilots and instructors.

So what is "the fighter pilot's view?" Jaros explains precise techniques for establishing and maintaining aircraft control in an engine-out glide. He introduces General Aviation pilots to the USAF concept of Critical Action Procedures (CAPs), the "bold print" steps of emergency checklists that pilots must commit to memory and practice because there isn't time to reference the printed checklist when the need for executing CAPs arises. Using insider "pilot speak" and drawing on his military experience as well as test-flying his Beechcraft Bonanza, he addresses specific techniques for optimizing glide and ground path with changes in airplane weight, wind and airplane configuration. Jaros presents a thorough explanation of energy management as it relates to glide angle and path. He provides tips for deriving CAPs from the Pilot's Operating Handbook emergency checklists since most light airplane procedures do not highlight the critical memory steps, prioritizing those steps based on the real-world causes of recoverable engine failures.

Applying his extensive fighter pilot experience to handing engine failures in General Aviation airplanes, Jaros explores numerous considerations not often developed in pilot training or instructional manuals, including:

- Effects of various propeller speeds on glide performance
- Emphasis on attempting to restart a failed engine for as long as the attempt makes sense
- Techniques for the engine-out flare
- The "gear up or gear down" question about off-airport landings
- Dealing with engine failure while in Instrument Meteorological Conditions

Jaros concludes his book with a section on engine-out training and practice basics. He suggests various techniques he has tested for safely simulating engine-out glides.

As Jaros notes, when faced with surviving an engine failure in a single-engine airplane "it all boils down to *you and your currency*" on engine-out and engine restart procedures.

Engine Out Survival Tactics: Fighter Pilot Tactics for General Aviation Engine Loss Emergencies will give you the tools you need to design a training regimen to develop and maintain critical engine failure survival skills.

Thomas P. Turner – *Executive Director, American Bonanza Society Air Safety Foundation*

PREFACE

"I learned the discipline of flying in order to have the freedom of flight....Discipline prevents crashes."
- Captain John Cook, British Airways, Concorde Pilot

General Aviation (GA) aircraft accidents kill hundreds of people every year. These crashes and fatalities have always been a source of much discussion, and a source of much study. Amidst all of the statistic and analysis, engine power loss and mechanical failure mishaps continue to be a leading cause of fatal accidents in General Aviation. In fact, engine loss accidents are the number one cause of crashes not later deemed as "pilot error."

How can we better prepare pilots for these types of failures, the types of failures that are out of their control and in which no one can see coming? With this book, and some training, I aim to help you become a more informed and safer pilot. You will be armed with the tactics to defeat the engine loss situation in your single engine aircraft, and survive.

A fact sheet issued by the FAA in 2014 stated that powerplant system component failure was the third leading cause for all General Aviation fatalities for the decade 2001 – 2011 (FAA Fact Sheet, 30 Jul 2014). Only loss of control inflight and controlled flight into terrain (CFIT) have a higher fatality rate.

Why are engine loss accidents and fatality rates so high? Are not all pilots well trained and well versed in handling emergencies, especially with an emergency as significant as losing an engine? Loss of an engine inflight is a significant event, a serious emergency, especially for a single engine airplane. Interestingly enough, while not totally avoidable, and certainly unpredictable, this emergency is one that can have a catastrophic outcome or a totally safe outcome. There are people who have lost their engine in General Aviation single engine aircraft, and are still here to talk about it. Yet there are also incredible statistics of fatalities for the same. Why are there such polar opposites regarding this particular emergency procedure?

According to the FAA, an Advisory Circular issued 15 Jun 1998 on reciprocating engine power-loss accident prevention and trend monitoring disclosed that the overall trend of engine loss accidents had basically remained the same as that of the 1960s. Of 1,007 engine related accidents reviewed from 1994 through 1996 "518 or 51% of the accidents were attributed to pilot error, such as poor [engine] preflight planning, inspection, or improper use of engine controls. 302 accidents or 30% were attributed to mechanical failure such as valve or cylinder failure, and the remaining 187 accidents or 19% were attributed to improper [engine] maintenance and/ or inspection of the aircraft" (FAA AC 20-105B, Jun 1998). I'd also like to emphasize here that the above 51% includes fuel starvation and fuel mismanagement incidents as well.

Let me reiterate the above quotation. In over 1,000 engine failure accidents in a three year timeframe, every one of them resulted in some kind of engine-out situation and possibly subsequent bending of metal or bruising of egos!

I'd like to think that I (or you) as professional and conscientious pilots could eliminate just about all of those accident variables by fueling correctly, preflighting correctly, and having excellent engine maintenance and care of any airplane we fly. Obviously, all of these dangers are not totally escapable or avoidable, especially for the rental fleet. However I would like to think that they are, and that *I personally* could catch and stop an imminent engine emergency by conducting better preflighting and fueling operations. Additionally, with some of today's engine analyzers and avionics, it is quite possible to catch "telltale" signs of impending engine trouble, or at least the trends in engine performance if one is diligent with his or her engine data downloads. There are tools and methods available to today's pilot that can increase one's engine health knowledge a fair amount. Theoretically, engine loss events could be a thing of the past. This is plausible, yet engine failures and accidents continue to occur every day.

Are pilots becoming safer? The Air Safety Institute reported in 2014 that total General Aviation accidents (of all types) in 2013 fell "by an unprecedented 18% from the year before, dropping below 1,000 for the first time. This improvement continued with a further 3% decrease to an all-time low of 923 in 2014" (ASI Scorecard, 2014). They also confirmed that these rates were not due to a decrease in flight activity.

So things might be improving from the "dark days" of the late-nineties. We also find that recently, 2011 was one of the safest years on record. "Documented mechanical failures or errors in aircraft maintenance caused 12% of all non-commercial fixed-wing accidents in 2011, including 7% of the fatal accidents. Both figures were at or near historic lows: The total of 147 [aircraft mechanical failures] was the smallest in the modern era, while 15 fatal accidents is just one more than the record [low] of 14 set in 2005" (Nall Report, 2011).

Are things trending toward recovery for overall GA safety? Perhaps. The fact still remains that pilots can unexpectedly lose their engine inflight, and there is nothing anyone can do about that. Historical statistics say that about 25-30% of the engine related accidents were just pure mechanical failures. Or as we sometimes like to say "the hatch just blew!" Of that 25-30% pure mechanical failure rate, there is nothing that you, or a CFI, or even Bob Hoover could have done about it had they been in the air that day. It just wasn't their day and the engine was going to fail no matter what was done in the pre-flight, fueling, or the maintenance beforehand. That is a pretty scary statistic if you ask me.

A recent independent study done by Cirrus Aircraft enthusiast and operator Mr. Joe Kirby looked at just Cirrus SR-22 and Bonanza A/G36 accidents from January 2010 through December 2014. He carefully went through the NTSB database and created his own incredible spreadsheet (available on the Engine Out webpage) which detailed every SR-22 and Bonanza 36 accident and its cause during that four year span. For these two specific airframes, over the specified timeframe, Mr. Kirby found that the number of engine mechanical failures were similar for both aircraft. He discovered that for each air-craft about 20% of the accidents were caused by pure mechan-ical engine failure (personal communication, March 2016). Interestingly, he also found nearly identical results to the above FAA Fact Sheet with regards to pilot loss of control and impact into terrain.

Of note, Mr. Kirby found fuel mismanagement statistics were markedly higher in Bonanza aircraft and accounted for nearly 24% of accidents, while Cirrus fuel mismanagement statistics accounted for just 4% of accidents for that aircraft. Generally speaking, fuel mismanagement accident statistics have decreased across the fleet from 8% of all GA accidents in 2002, to 5% of all accident caused in 2012 (Nall Reports, 2013 & 2003).

But enough statistics for now, let us change gears for a minute and talk about something related, the engine out emergency.

If you are like most pilots, you have received what you probably perceive as an adequate level of engine out training in your GA single engine aircraft. In my opinion, this engine loss training as well as the level of understanding for a majority of GA pilots and CFIs is severely lacking. Why do I say that?

It wasn't until I completed USAF pilot training and attained over 2,000 hours in fighters and fighter-type aircraft that I realized the extreme difference between GA and the military with regards to emergency training and specifically, engine out training. I am not saying that all CFIs are cowboys and cavalier about this type of schooling. I'm also not implying that all GA pilots are unskilled in this area. Many GA pilots are highly competent, but unfortunately, that is not always the case. Airplanes continue to lose engines and people still lose lives every week due to crashes following engine power loss. I know that most CFIs do happen to teach some kind of engine out training, however, I will offer that this training is grossly inadequate, and the average GA pilot's currency (i.e., practice) in engine out training is just as equally underwhelming.

Most of my GA engine out training (back in the day!) was simply the CFI pulling my throttle to idle and then instructing me on how to find a landing spot and what was the best glide speed for whatever aircraft we were training in that day. Seldom did we ever address restarts, checklists procedures, Critical Action Procedures (CAPs), or the more advanced thoughts on energy management, drag management, sight pictures and touchdown planning. I believe the average GA student and certainly the private or commercial single engine pilot *needs* to know some of these key concepts.

Additionally, when was the last time your CFI asked you to go practice engine out procedures? Most of mine never really did, or do. If you are practicing engine out procedures today, good on ya! If you are a CFI, are you teaching these advanced concepts? Or are you just pulling the throttle, announcing "engine failure" and then doing a simple glide to some point on the earth with little or no further discussion with your student?

What about this, does the following drill sound familiar? Maybe you had a CFI "kill your engine" on a recent BFR or a checkout of some kind. "Now pick a landing site," he or she said. You diligently found a field or some road during the "procedure" and executed a glide to it with a go around as you neared the open field. You managed to make it to the field and execute a go around. You felt pretty good about that actually.

Success! you think to yourself; you have been trained in engine out procedures! Easy as lemon pie right?

Well, no not really, I am being sarcastic. What I hope to impart upon you is not the inadequacies of your CFI and the training you received, but instead point out where some of that training has fallen short, and what all GA pilots need to be prepared for while instilling a further sense of the knowledge and factors that all contribute to a successful engine out scenario and a successful recovery. Unfortunately, most GA engine out training is deficient and lacking some of the basics that every pilot needs. Simply pulling the throttle to idle and holding best glide speed will not be ample practice for most GA pilots, especially new or inexperienced pilots, and maybe for some of our more seasoned flyers too. There is so much more to engine loss training.

As an ex-military fighter pilot, I recall the incredible amount of training I went through in my single engine airplane to prepare me for all kinds of emergencies, and especially the engine out situation. Not only did we learn and prepare for losing our one-and-only engine in the aircraft, but we regularly continued to train for losing that engine as well. And we even had an "ace up our sleeve" …the ejection seat! If things *really* got bad, well the ole ejection seat was always there to save us from certain doom…right? Even so, we trained heavily for the engine out situation and even had to demonstrate one all the way to the landing flare during our recurring check rides.

In fighters, we also maintained a currency for practice engine out scenarios. One a month minimum to be exact, or twelve a year was the minimum number to have logged "in the books." We also had a 90-day currency. What that means is that every pilot was required to go out and actually practice an engine out profile at those intervals. Failure to do so or to meet that required currency would lead to additional training with an instructor pilot and could also even ground the individual if he or she was significantly overdue. We took engine out practice very seriously…and the USAF did as well. These currencies and training rules were heavily documented and described in various regulations and paper guidance that we were required to follow.

This book is designed from a fighter pilot's view of engine out training. I am not attempting to offer a military-like training regimen for GA pilots, nor am I suggesting that all GA pilots "fit into the mold" of a military style training course. Nor do I "know it all" or pretend to know it all. My hope, for this book is simply to attempt to impart upon you, the GA pilot, some of the ways in which we trained for emergencies (specifically the engine out scenario) in the military in hopes that you can follow a similar course for your own training, and ultimately make all GA pilots well-versed and thus safer when it comes to engine loss in flight. This book will give you a new bag of tricks and tactics, all designed to help you overcome an engine out situation, but the willingness and desire to go practice this stuff…is up to you.

You will not become Chuck Yeager after reading this book. However, after reading this book you will probably know way more than your average GA pilot about engine loss scenarios and recoveries, maybe even more than your CFI. If you are a CFI, you will be able to add even more realism and relevance to your teachings.

My desires are that you take your time to digest this book and then go out and apply and practice some of these techniques in your single engine aircraft of choice. Quite possibly (and hopefully) this writing will teach you some new techniques, and optimistically it can become a good source of reference for you as you continue to advance your pilot skill sets. By reading this book and taking measures to address your own training for emergencies and engine out situations, you have taken the first step to becoming a safer GA pilot. I applaud you!

Lastly, while this book is designed for the General Aviation pilot in any single engine airplane, we will be focusing our studies, charts, and procedures on one specific aircraft, the Beech Bonanza. Even though some of these examples and procedures are Bonanza specific, please realize that all of the following procedures *may* be used in any single engine aircraft. While glide ratios and speeds and so forth might be different than in your particular aircraft of choice, the concepts and facts all still apply. Some minor adjustments to your procedures and numbers will of course be needed, however we will generally focus on the Bonanza to keep things simple. I will also do my best to keep this book "math free." If you are like me, math is a challenge, even at one G and zero knots! Where applicable, I'll have the math accomplished and illustrated for you to review.

So I will conclude by answering one of my above questions. When I stated 'There are people who have lost their engine in General Aviation single engine aircraft, and are still here to talk about it. Yet there are also incredible statistics of fatalities for the same. *Why* are there such polar opposites regarding this particular emergency procedure?'

I believe the answer is training and knowledge. Training and knowledge are what will save you from an engine loss situation (and any emergency actually). If you are a pilot, or a CFI, looking to expand your engine out knowledge and training repertoire, this book is for you.

I hope you enjoy it, and I sincerely hope you learn from it!

~ Buster

INTRODUCTION

---

*"If you're faced with a forced landing, fly the
thing as far into the crash as possible."*

- Bob Hoover

You've just leveled off at 10,500 feet MSL in your normally
aspirated Single Engine V-tail Bonanza. It's a beautiful
day, and you are looking forward to the flight. There are some
scattered clouds below you, but you're VFR and the weather for
the trip should be good all along the entire route, according to
your exceptional mission planning. The NOTAMs all look fine,
and you are not really expecting anything too complicated for
the basically routine one hour flight you have planned.

Today you've got your significant other aboard. Although she's a little nervous about flying in small planes, she puts up with it from time to time and enjoys short trips. It's way better than driving right?

You accomplish your level off, reduce the prop RPM and start to get the big ole Bonanza trimmed up for cruise flight. The engine monitor helps you comfortably set the engine parameters. Today you'll fine tune the mixture for peak EGTs as you are looking for the best performance and speed for that altitude. After a few minutes, you have the engine set nicely, the trim comfortably set and you engage the autopilot, so you can do a few other administrative tasks and such. It's a great day to be flying!

You are setting up something on the GPS when a flicker catches your eye on the engine monitor. Upon further investigation you notice a high CHT on the number five cylinder. That seems odd you think (that cylinder usually likes to run cooler than the rest). You monitor the CHT and start to feel what seems to be a slight vibration in the seat of your pants. Maybe that's just the prop not being so smooth, or most likely your increased awareness levels are just fabricating these anomalies in your mind. Maybe.

No! There is definitely a vibration.

Then it happens. BANG! A very loud and perceivable concussion hits the aircraft. You feel a deceleration and notice the RPM is no longer where you set it earlier; it's quite a bit lower. The engine surges, and a slapping and banging sounds begin to get audible along with a terrific shudder and vibration through the airframe and into your seat. You can now hardly read the instruments as the vibration has turned your airplane into a paint-shaker! You smell the unmistakable and pungent smell of fuel.

Airspeed is bleeding off...the propeller grinds to a halt. The shudders and shakes go away, and it's now noticeably quiet in the cockpit, except for the sound of air slipping past the windows and doors and a slight crackle on the radio.

You have just lost the engine!

This is a very real situation that you will need to be prepared for. Are you ready? No, really, are you ready?

In 2013, the NTSB calculated that there were over 150 powerplant malfunction-related accidents in General Aviation that year alone. This was the second leading cause for non-fatal accident totals, and the leading cause for all types of accidents when non-fatal and fatal accidents were combined across all categories (NTSB, 2013). Historically, some of these powerplant-related accidents were from fuel associated issues, or poor preflight checks, but generally 30% are attributed to mechanical engine failures themselves (FAA AC 20-105B, Jun 1998).

What kind of training have YOU had in engine out procedures? Are you even current in engine out practice? Wait a minute. There is no FAA prescribed currency for engine out procedures or practice. What are you talking about Buster? Well, maybe there should be.

When is the last time YOU really thought about the glide numbers, and your actions following an engine out situation? Do you have the procedures in your checklist committed to memory?

Hopefully the above fictional scenario never happens to you. But if it does (or even if you have just a sick engine that might be able to limp along) I want you to be prepared and armed with the knowledge and tactics to safely recover the aircraft.

What about you? Are you ready to take your engine out training to the next level?

GLIDE BASICS

"Nothing said I had to crash." - Bob Hoover

In this chapter we are going to dig into the glide and the glide mechanics of your single engine machine. We will specifically be discussing the Bonanza, and I will attempt to cite data and differences if there are any for the 35 (V-tail) series or the 36 (straight tail, six-seater) series. Realize that all these Bonanza planes are different actually, with different model year changes, fuselage lengths, weights, and so on. The 36 Bonanza has a much longer fuselage and the wings are even mounted slightly farther aft than your typical four-seat V-tail or four-seat straight tail Bonanza. Some Bonanza's are highly modified. Some are stripped down for lightness and speed.

But ultimately, they are all quite similar in system design, and they do share the same wing. Some differences in the numbers and procedures do exist, and I will attempt to highlight those where applicable.

Regardless, I want you to understand that even though these specific Bonanza aircraft will be covered, the procedures and physics for gliding and executing an engine out scenario will be similar for any GA single engine aircraft. The "laws of flight" do not change between the humble Piper Cub and the big and beautiful Boeing 747. While the glide numbers and descent rates for say a Cessna 182 or an RV-8 will be different from our Bonanza, the topics covered and the basics we'll highlight will apply just as much to those aircraft. If you are a Cessna driver or a Mooney operator, or even fly a 1936 Stearman, the intent of this writing is to help you better prepare for that day your engine fails.

Some of this information is quite basic and usually taught very early in civilian and military flight training. That being said, I would still like to take the time in this chapter to cover some of these basics. Even if you think you have all this well learned and understood, take a few minutes to hang with me and refresh on these basic ideas.

I'm also going to use some of my military background training and vernacular as we go along. Of course that in its essence is why I'm writing this book. I am drawing a lot from the fighter pilot ways of doing business, and also comparing it to General Aviation. I tend to compare the two when I fly. Sometimes I even fly and train in my humble Bonanza today in a similar fashion to how we did it in USAF Fighter Squadrons.

Let's define and discuss a few of these terms now so you have a frame of reference:

FO. FO stands for Flameout. In jet aircraft, when the engine quits, we generally refer to this as a flameout. Technically speaking, a flameout means the jet engine has lost its flame, or its source of ignition. Even though the engine might have stopped turning due to a blade failure or bird ingestion, or some other mechanical breakdown (think "Sully" Sullenberger in the Hudson River, January 2009) we still refer to it as a flameout. Essentially, anytime the jet engine stops working, we call it a flameout just for the sake of conversation and vernacular.

SFO. SFO stands for Simulated Flameout. This is a practice maneuver where we set engine power to idle (and employ other drag devices as well) and pretend that the engine quit for some reason. We will discuss the particulars of the SFO in a later chapter, but basically, the SFO is a practice maneuver used for training in engine out emergencies. There are also different kinds of SFOs.

Wire. A wire is simply a glide path. If you are flying a three degree ILS approach, you are on a "three wire." In the F-16 we had many different dive angles and glide paths for many different approaches and weapons deliveries. The term "wire" is simply a term used when discussing these dive angles.

For instance, when planning a 45 degree nose-low weapons delivery, it became easier to visualize an actual wire, or string, from the target up into space at a 45 degree angle versus planning and talking about it as a glide path. This also makes it easy to visualize your position relative to the wire, which is critical to the weapon delivery or any nose low glide path type maneuver. But simply quantified the wire is a desired glide path. Visualization of your position relative to that wire is an important concept, and we'll dig into that in a later chapter.

Energy. Energy and energy management in aircraft are basically the combination of altitude and airspeed. I'm sure you already understand this relationship and that being high and fast gives you a much different energy situation than when you are low and slow. Like all energy in the universe, energy cannot be created or destroyed, but only traded.

We'll take a little bit more in depth look at energy and how it relates to airplanes and the engine out scenario in a future chapter, but one good energy management example was ole Bob Hoover. Recall Bob Hoover and his Aero Commander Shrike twin, pulling into the vertical for a loop, cutting both engines to off, completing the loop, and landing and taxiing in under no engine power to a designated stopping point on the field! Ole Bob had an amazing understanding of energy and energy management.

Glide Ratio

What *is* a glide ratio? Simply stated, a glide ratio is the mathematical ratio of how far forward an airplane travels under no power, and its subsequent vertical distance lost in traveling that forward distance. Generally, these ratios are given for stabilized flight, stabilized at that airplane's "best glide" airspeed and under no wind conditions.

According to the Pilot Operating Handbook (POH), the Bonanza has a clean glide ratio of about 10 to 1. Specifically, the POH (33, 35 & 36 series) states that the Bonanza, when clean (gear up, flaps up, cowl flaps closed and propeller pitch set to coarse) will glide 1.7 nm (2 sm) forward for every 1,000 feet of altitude. What this means is that for every 1.7 nm of forward travel in a glide the aircraft will lose 1,000 vertical feet of altitude. Doing a little math gives us the 10 to 1 glide ratio numbers that are used and debated quite often.

Every aircraft's glide ratio is different of course. According to aircraft builder Grob, their Grob 103 glider has a glide ratio of 36 to 1. That's pretty good! The Grob sailplane can glide forward 36 miles for every mile vertical, or it can glide 36,000 feet forward for every 1,000 feet vertical. The F-16 has a glide ratio of nearly 8 to 1, (7nm/5k feet according to the dash 1). Not quite as good as a Grob sailplane or a Bonanza, but a little better than a brick thrown off an overpass.

Aircraft weight, wing loading, and wing design all play a significant role in how an aircraft will glide. Discussion into that is far beyond the scope of this book. However it is important to understand the basics and that glide ratio is simply how far forward the aircraft can travel and how much distance downward, or altitude, that forward travel will require.

Glide ratio is generally quite stable and fixed for each aircraft, but it can vary slightly depending on aircraft airspeed and weight. As far as weight goes when looking at two theoretically identical aircraft, a heavier aircraft will have a higher rate of descent, but its airspeed must increase to offset this higher rate of descent in gliding flight. This higher rate of descent and subsequent increased speed simply makes the aircraft "go faster" and descend faster, (and eventually hit the ground *sooner* than a comparable aircraft that is lightly loaded) but the overall glide *ratio* will remain unchanged between the two aircraft. So a heavier aircraft must glide at a faster indicated airspeed, however the glide ratio and touchdown spot will not change from an identical aircraft that is lighter.

One of the most important parts of aircraft wing design is Lift to Drag ratio, also known as L/D or L/D Ratio. This is sometimes spoken as "L over D." The L/D is the amount of lift a wing develops as it moves through the air, divided by the drag it creates while doing so. Building a wing or aircraft with a high L/D is generally more desirable by engineers as this equates to increased fuel economy and climb performance. Figure

1 shows a sample L/D chart, also called a polar curve. Note that the point where the tangent line from the origin touches the curved plot is the speed which corresponds to Best Glide speed. This is where the aircraft is producing the most amount of lift and the least amount of drag.

L/D Chart

Figure 1

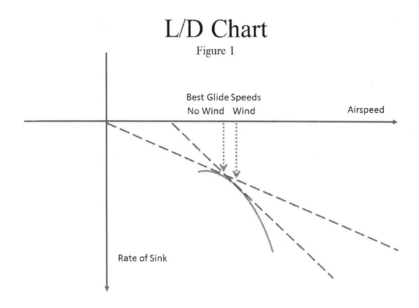

Additionally, this most efficient best glide airspeed at L/D also equates to a set AoA. The AoA that corresponds to best L/D will never change, regardless of altitude, airspeed, weight, or air temperature. If you have an AoA indicator, you should be able to determine with a quick flight test what AoA corresponds to your best glide airspeed. More on AoA in the Training and Practice chapter.

Wind Effects on Glide Ratio

Wind is an important component on the actual gliding distance for aircraft, and understanding wind and its effect on glide performance are paramount. The chief factor for winds and their effects is understanding that winds aloft change groundspeed, even in a glide. Increased or decreased headwinds or tailwinds affect that groundspeed and thus the subsequent gliding distance of an aircraft. If you think about it, wind is effectively changing the glide ratio. Remember, that with increased headwinds and tailwinds, the *time* in your glide will not change, only just how far you can go.

Sailplane pilots talk about the effects of wind on their performance quite a bit. They have a common Rule of Thumb (ROT) which states that you should increase or decrease your indicated airspeed with a headwind or tailwind by half of the wind component. So a glider soaring along at say 100 KIAS (best L/D) finds himself with a 10 knot headwind, he would need to increase his speed by 5 knots for optimum L/D. This makes sense. If you look at the polar curve in figure 1, you can see the steeper second dashed line already "has some airspeed." So it starts higher to the right on the Airspeed line for its "origin" and contacts the L/D polar curve at a higher value on the curved plot. I cannot locate a solid L/D chart for our Bonanzas, so I do not know if this ROT holds true for us.

What about distance traveled? How far can you go, or how much distance would you gain or lose in a glide with a headwind or tailwind? Crunching some numbers on this gives us some interesting relationships. First remember that your "factory set" glide ratio has and will not change, and therefore your time in the glide will not change with winds. Remember that a large headwind or tailwind will not change the *time* in your glide; it will only change just how far you can travel.

So assuming that the headwind or tailwind component is constant throughout the gliding profile, and disregarding any TAS effects, we can come up with some interesting ROT for headwind and tailwind effects on the glide. For example, if you are at 10,000 AGL, we know that you can optimally glide 17 nm (1.7 nm per every 1,000 feet of altitude). If we academically say that we are gliding at 100 knots groundspeed (KGS), and now we have constant 10 knot headwind, we will now see 90 KGS, but the same time aloft. Figuring distance by multiplying speed by time, now gives us a distance travelled of 15.3 nm. That distance is exactly 1.7 nm shorter than our no-wind glide distance from 10,000 feet! The relationship works for 10, 20, 30 etc. knots of headwind or tailwind, and each 10 knots reduces or improves our subsequent glide distance by 1.7 nm when starting at 10,000 feet AGL.

The relationship also works at 5,000 AGL. But because a lower aircraft is exposed to the wind effects for a shorter time-frame, the resulting wind effects and distances traveled are less.

Crunching the numbers for a 5,000 AGL aircraft yield exactly half of the above figures, or 0.85 nm for every 10 knots of headwind or tailwind. Likewise, from 20,000 feet AGL, the relationship doubles from our 10,000 foot example. But remember, these numbers are fairly academic, as it will be tough to predict headwind and tailwind components at all altitudes, as they tend to change heading and velocity at various altitudes, however, we can use the ROT to get a rough estimate of their effects when planning.

An accurate estimation of one's glide performance with a headwind or tailwind could be stated as the distance change (Δ "delta") equals glide ratio distance per 10 knots per 10,000 feet.

Distance Δ = Glide Ratio distance at 10kts/10k

Drag

So what can you, the pilot do about your "factory set" glide performance? Not much unfortunately. The engineers and the laws of physics have basically set those performance parameters for you. Unless you can find a way to shed a lot of weight, while airborne, your glide profile or angle will basically be relatively unchanged. Even then, recall that weight equates to vertical speed, so the best you could do by shedding weight would be to slow your descent and buy yourself more time before the crash. But unfortunately, your glide performance (glide ratio) will basically remain unchanged.

Figure 2 shows a basic total drag curve. This plot for your aircraft will help you determine what your best speed is for minimum drag, which will help you attain best glide distance. That speed is at the bottom of the total drag curve. Note that as airspeed increases, form drag (or parasite drag) increases. As speed decreases, more induced drag is created as the wing now develops the equivalent lift at a slower speed (because AoA increases).

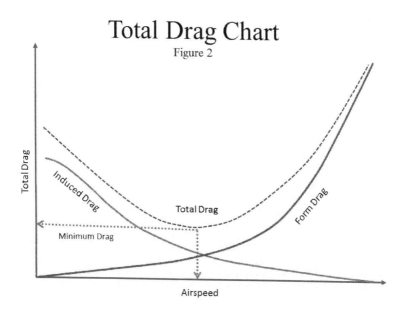

Total Drag Chart
Figure 2

However, drag is one thing you can control that affects your glide dramatically. One of the key factors in any glide, for any airplane, is reducing drag. Sailplane or glider aircraft go to great lengths to decrease drag in their design phase. Increased drag slows the aircraft. The pilot of a really 'draggy' airplane would have to lower the nose to regain best glide speed and thus change the glide ratio for the worse. Think of it like a parachute. There is so much drag on the parachute that the glide ratio becomes effectively zero to 1, and the object under the chute travels straight down. This option is not generally available for the GA single engine aircraft, except for a few noted examples like the Cirrus.

Some single engine aircraft do not have much in the way of drag control. I remember my early training days in the local airpark's crusty and old (but reliable) Cessna 150. That old gal was pretty draggy from the chocks, and as a newbie pilot in training, once my CFI pulled the power and carburetor heat, there wasn't much else to do but look down for a landing spot and watch the world rise.

However in the Bonanza and quite a few more powerful single engine aircraft, we do have some good drag devices at our disposal. Cowl flaps for instance. Cowl flaps are used to aid in engine cooling, which is a good thing normally. Especially in the climb. But once established in level cruise flight, with the engine at a comfortable temperature, most pilots close the cowl flaps to help gain speed. Cowl flaps don't have much drag when extended in the Bonanza, but every aircraft with them will be different. If you have lost the engine, every bit of extra "slickness" and speed you can gain may help make the difference between a successful engine out landing or not.

The landing gear are also a huge source of drag, obviously. Some aircraft have fixed gear, and some do not. The Bonanza has the advantage of retractable gear, which is nice for gliding performance. But having the gear up can also be a disadvantage as well when it's time to lower them, especially during an emergency. We'll deliberate landing techniques later, and whether it's preferable to leave the gear up or put them down during an engine out scenario. Landing gear can also be a great way to add drag, when you need it. When you find yourself high on energy during a glide, you have the advantage of dropping the gear, increasing drag, and thus steepening up your descent to the landing spot.

Flaps. Flaps are an interesting subject of debate for engine out practice and glide ratios. Flaps do increase lift, but they also increase drag, typically. Typical flaps on most GA single engine aircraft can be a huge source of drag depending on how far they are extended. In your average General Aviation single engine aircraft "flap deflection of up to 15° primarily produces lift with minimal drag. Flap deflection beyond 15° produces a large increase in drag" (FAASafety.gov).

With flaps however, the issue quickly becomes glide speed and flap maximum speed proximity. For the Bonanza, at best glide speed of 105 KIAS, (110 KIAS for the A36) that is below the maximum flap extension speed of 123 KIAS (117 KIAS S/N D-8871 and earlier), but not by much. The difference is just 18 knots (12 knots for older V-tails). Maximum flap speeds are just one knot faster for the A36 at a full 30 degrees, putting the A36 at 14 knots between best glide speed and maximum flap deflection speed. Ultimately, all of the above Bonanza specific flap and glide speeds are pretty close in proximity.

Use of flaps for glides is generally frowned upon. When we execute a glide, either in practice or in a real engine out situation, there will be times when the pilot needs to trade in some altitude for airspeed. In an effort to reduce altitude, sometimes the pilot will lower the nose and subsequently pick up too much speed. Without other ample drag sources, one can easily over-speed the flaps and possibly cause more damage to the already wounded airplane.

It's easy to do, and easy to lose track of maximum flap speeds when practicing, and flap position will certainly be one of the last things on your mind when faced with a real engine emergency.

Personally, I am not a fan of using flaps for drag as the airspeed limits for my flaps are too close to my best glide speed, and my POH doesn't recommend it for gliding. You should compare the flap and glide speeds for your aircraft now. More on *when* to use flaps later.

What about propeller control for drag? Well, of course. If you have a variable pitched propeller, you might be able to pull the prop lever back, thus reducing the blade angle of attack to the relative wind and reduce drag further. A fixed pitch propeller does not have this capability, unfortunately, and the pilot of this aircraft is stuck with a blade pitch as set by the factory. This "fine" or high pitch setting in the fixed pitch prop is good when the engine is producing power. This translates to a higher RPM, which is generally what we want for takeoff, climb, and sometimes cruise flight.

I like to think of that high pitch setting (either by design or by having the prop lever forward in a variable speed propeller) as "first gear" in a car. For those that know how to drive a stick shift or "manual" car, you know what it's like to drive in first gear. How sensitive is the speed of the vehicle to throttle? It's reactive, right? When driving in first gear and you then come off the pedal, the car rapidly decelerates and everyone lurches forward. You probably remember doing something similar during your early stick-shift driver training, and maybe what your dad said to you right after you did that maneuver!

It's the same thing with airplane propellers. With the prop lever forward, it's like being in first gear. It's great for accelerating, and climbing, but when you reduce the throttle the vehicle rapidly decelerates.

With the variable pitch propeller, pull the propeller lever back, and you get what is referred to as a coarse setting and the blade angles become closer to streamlined with the wind. This is an important concept to understand when it comes to your systems knowledge and ways to reduce drag. You will need to figure out for your individual aircraft what is required to move the prop lever aft and get a coarse pitch propeller. Most GA single engine aircraft require oil pressure to allow for the propeller hub to actually "actuate" and twist to different pitch settings. We will discuss more on this topic in a minute.

So is glide ratio important to you as a pilot "in the seat" of your single engine bird? Is it important to know that your aircraft has a glide ratio of 10 to 1 while you are flying around? Well, not really. That's not to say you shouldn't know and understand the concept of glide ratio, and maybe even know the numbers. But what is far more important and even critical to you the pilot is the numbers you'll use in the cockpit. I would be excited to meet someone that told me the glide ratio of their RV-8 was about 7 to 1, or whatever number they came up with. But in reality we pilots need to know our glide ratio in physical numbers that we can "see," use, and understand in the cockpit.

From the Bonanza checklist and POH, we know that the aircraft can glide (at best glide speed, clean) and get 1.7 nm per every thousand feet of altitude. You will need to dig into your POH and maybe even do some math (sorry) to figure out what the best glide speed of your aircraft will yield for distance travelled and altitude lost. A simple glide ratio is not enough for planning and flying an engine out scenario. You will need to translate that into thousands of vertical feet and most likely nautical miles travelled. Pilot-friendly references!

We will deliberate training for engine out scenarios in a future chapter. It will become imperative that you learn how to fly an engine out aircraft and what that sight picture, wire and sink rate or vertical velocity (VV) look like, both clean and dirty. But for now, a basic understanding of your aircraft's glide numbers is a good start.

You don't know what your airplane's numbers are? Go find them out now! Additionally, below are some typical glide distances (no wind) for some common single engine GA aircraft. These are POH numbers, so your real-world findings might be a little different. Please reference your POH for exact figures.

Aircraft	nm / 1,000 feet AGL	Approx Angle
RV-8	1.2 nm	7.8
RV-7, C-172, J3 Cub, C-T210	1.5 nm	6.2
C-152, SR-22, PA28-181	1.6 nm	5.8
Bonanza, Mooney	1.7 nm	5.5
PA28-140	1.9 nm	4.9
Cessna TTX, Navion (some)	2.0 nm	4.7

Weight

Remember how earlier we discussed aircraft weight and the glide? We said that weight and being lighter simply decreases our time until hitting the ground. Recall that the overall glide ratio will not change with a change in aircraft weight, just that time that it takes to fly the glide and impact the ground. However, it is worth taking a minute here to explore this in a little more depth. While the above still holds true, it is also good to understand that the weight of an aircraft also affects its best L/D airspeed.

But earlier, we said that on a given Total Drag plot, the lowest point on the total drag line equates to an airspeed, and that speed equates to the lowest drag airspeed. So how does airspeed change with weight and why would a heavier (or lighter) aircraft have different best glide airspeeds?

The answer is simple. Note in figure 3 below, that when aircraft weight is plotted against an L/D chart, the whole plot "slides" down and to the right. Higher weight necessitates a greater sink rate and thus a higher airspeed.

Weight
Figure 3

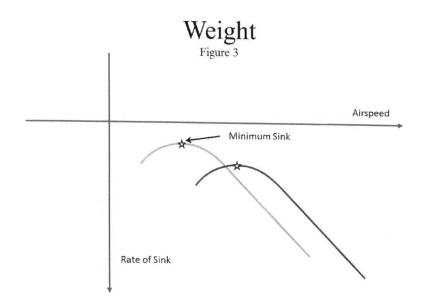

Not all airplanes are created equal, and each will behave differently for a given shift in weight. But it's important to remember that most manuals and factory guidance will list the airplane's best glide speed at only one set weight, typically max gross weight. I don't know about you, but it's not very often that I fly at maximum gross weight.

So what is your actual best glide airspeed when you are lighter than max gross? Some instructors will say it doesn't matter. They might also say that when confronted with an emergency engine out situation, the airspeed difference is so negligible that it makes no difference. I'd like to argue differently. But let us take a look at the Bonanza and how weight affects our best glide speed.

A little research will show that most V speeds for all aircraft are affected by aircraft weight. Vx and Vy, as well as Va are all directly affected by gross weight. There is a common rule of thumb that applies to most GA singles that states that V speeds can be adjusted one knot per 100 pounds of aircraft weight. As a rule, this approximation is somewhat accurate, but be careful, it's not exact. Actual changes in airspeed can be slightly more or less than one knot, and you might want to know the specifics before you go out and attempt to "gnat's ass it" …as they say.

For most GA aircraft, a much more accurate weight and glide speed calculation is needed. Glide speed changes *more than* one knot per 100 pounds of weight. The following formula in figure 4 can be used for any aircraft to determine how weight affects best glide speed.

Figure 4

$$\sqrt{\frac{New\ Weight}{Gross\ Weight}} \times \text{Gross Weight Best Glide Speed}$$

$$\sqrt{\frac{3000}{3400}} \times 105 = 98.6$$

So for a V35 Bonanza with a max gross weight of 3,400 pounds and a POH best glide speed of 105 KIAS at that max gross weight, we can now find the following for an example 3,000 pound Bonanza aircraft.

Our new best glide speed becomes 99 KIAS. It's worth noting here that our best glide speed changed by a little over 6 knots for a 400 pound reduction of weight. That is about 1.5 knots per 100 pounds. If you run the math for a 2,400 pound aircraft (1,000 pounds below gross) you get a new best glide speed of 88 KIAS. That is a 17 knot difference, or about 1.7 knots per 100 pounds. So the relationship is not linear for weight lost and airspeed decreased for best glide, but it is close. Clearly, more math is required when it comes to calculating best glide speeds, as the old theory of one knot per 100 pounds is not very accurate here.

Below is figure 5 with glide speed and weight calculations accomplished for our V35 and A36 Bonanzas.

Bonanza Weights & Best Glide
Figure 5

Weight	2000	2200	2400	2600	2800	3000	3200	3400	3600
V35 (KIAS)	81	85	88	92	95	99	102	105	N/A
A36 (KIAS)	82	86	90	94	97	100	104	107	110

I'd also recommend that you make a chart for your airplane of all your important V speeds and how they change for various common weights at which you fly. Of course, I would hope that you include glide speeds at various weights like the above chart and then use those speeds for real world flying and engine out glide training. While the speeds might just vary a knot or two depending on weight, it will be valuable to know those differences as it might make a difference someday in an actual situation. Additionally, you will find the above glide chart in the Bonanza Smart Card at the end of the book, and on the Engine Out webpage.

Personally, I have committed just three best glide speeds to memory. These speeds are the max gross airspeed that the POH lists, a "family on-board mid weight" speed and a "solo mid weight" speed. These work for me. You will need to do a little math and planning for your favorite single engine aircraft common glide speeds.

Propellers

Let's talk a little about propeller pitch and the infamous windmilling propeller. Understanding what the propeller blade angle or pitch is, is very important to optimizing your glide. It will also be important for you to look into what mechanical system drives the variable pitch propeller in your aircraft, or even if you have a variable pitch propeller or not. If you have a fixed pitch propeller, then you are unfortunately stuck with that blade pitch.

Most twin engine propeller airplanes have what is known as "full feathering" propellers. This is done by design to enable the twin driver to streamline the blades of a propeller to nearly parallel with the wind in case an engine fails. By doing this, the twin engine aircraft pilot can reduce propeller drag for the failed engine, and can rely on its other good engine to remain airborne (some twins have rather lethargic and underpowered engines, so the full feathering propeller is very important). The designers of these engines know that having blades flat, or perpendicular to the wind, will create a lot of drag as the propeller is turned due to the wind. This is known as windmilling.

Think of this as being similar to holding your hand out the window of a car. Aim the palm of your hand toward the wind and you can feel the drag. Turn your hand palm down and now your hand becomes streamlined and parallel with the wind, and you'll obviously feel far less drag.

So, single engine aircraft have either fixed pitch propellers or variable pitch propellers. If you fly your single engine airplane behind a variable pitch propeller, you have greater control over your propeller pitch, but in some instances you probably cannot fully feather the prop. In most systems, the propeller blades turn and change pitch with the use of (or absence of) oil and oil pressure. This is the same oil that circulates and moves through the engine pistons, cams, oil cooler, and the like. It is *critical* for you to know what type of system you are operating behind. For the Bonanzas, and our Continental engines, we need oil pressure to control the blade pitch, and for us, the default setting for the blades when there is no oil pressure is flat (also known as fine pitch), like your hand out the car window with your palm facing into the wind. We need oil pressure to twist the blades where we want them for various regimes of flight, otherwise they go flat and perpendicular to the airstream.

Why are they built this way? Well, it's because we only have one engine and typically just one oil system. If that oil system fails or loses oil and subsequently oil pressure, it's important that the blades automatically go to fine pitch (just like on takeoff or when full power is needed) and are able to provide maximum RPM and horsepower. If they went streamlined or coarse pitch with oil pressure loss, any combustive power remaining in the engine would not be able to generate any power or thrust from the blades when they are streamlined.

In a twin, the opposite is true, and this makes sense. In a twin, you will want your propeller blades to streamline or feather with an engine or oil system problem as it is assumed you have another good engine remaining. Not so much in a single engine airplane.

Some piston engines use other types of propeller pitch change mechanisms, and oil is not always the primary method of changing propeller pitch. Additionally, some systems that allow for a propeller to be feathered must also require the propeller blades to feather before the RPM drops below a certain value, because below this value the pitch mechanism will be unable to overcome the aerodynamic forces on the slowly turning or "frozen" propeller. You will need to figure out, for your aircraft, what kind of system you have that allows for twisting of the propeller blades, what its default setting is, and any system limitations.

Windmilling Propellers

So what is the big ole deal with a windmilling propeller? Why is that such a bad thing? Why do pilots always talk about engine out situations and the windmilling propeller?

Think of it this way. Imagine one of those maple tree seeds that looks like a propeller. Those fall and spin just like a windmilling propeller. They don't fall to the earth very fast, do they? They spin and spin and seem to fall and drift for quite a long time. That is because they produce a good bit of drag. Lots of drag in fact! If you find one someday, pick it up and strip away a half or so of its "propeller" wing surface. Give it a toss into the air and watch how it will now fall quite fast and probably not even spin much at all. That's because it doesn't create much drag without its "propeller."

The bottom line is that a windmilling propeller creates a lot of drag. Helicopters also use this phenomenon to their advantage when performing autorotation and landing after they lose their engine. By keeping energy and speed in the rotors, they effectively are windmilling them and that will slow the helicopter's descent. Like the maple seed.

The scientific reason behind all this is that as a spinning propeller spins it is producing drag all the way around the arc. Effectively, the rotating blade becomes a disc and retains the drag properties of that disc. Interestingly, if we look at the 1958 T-34A pilot manual it tells us that our glide distance can be increased by as much as 25% over the "normal" numbers with the propeller pulled back to coarse and not windmilling. The later 1982 Navy T-34B manual claims up to 30% increased glide distance by doing the same.

Figure 6 below shows a baseline chart for drag as it pertains to a windmilling or stationary propeller. Note that a windmilling propeller has much higher coefficient of drag until the pilot can get the blade angle further coarse and greater than about 20 degrees from perpendicular to the wind stream.

Windmilling Propeller
Figure 6

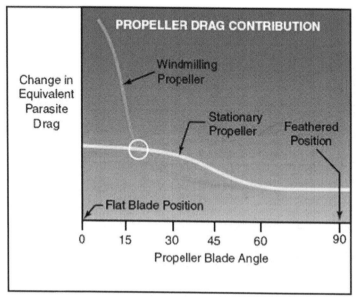

Image from FAA Special Airworthiness Information Bulletin, 2005

For you, the GA pilot, just understand that a windmilling propeller produces significant drag and that drag will significantly reduce your gliding distance. If faced with an engine out scenario, it is important to get that propeller "feathered" or to a significant coarse pitch, as soon as you can. Failure to do so will not be the end of the world, but your glide ratio will suffer. Additionally, your descent "sight picture" and glide angle will be different with a fine pitch flat and windmilling propeller. This is something to consider in your training. Knowing that your real-world engine out scenario sight-picture and descent gradient could be somewhat different for what you have trained for, is very important.

We will look at this a little more in the Training and Practice chapter as well as ways to add realism and accuracy to your engine out training.

In summary, we have looked at some (hopefully) fairly interesting and basic information on glides, glide performance and glide ratios. We have seen what system limitations contribute to gliding performance as well as some things that you the pilot can do to affect your particular aircraft's glide performance. All of which are very important baseline factors that you should understand when it comes to an aircraft glide and improving that glide should you ever need to do so.

So what happens when you actually have an emergency in your aircraft? Specifically, what happens when you have an engine out emergency in your normally trusty single engine bird? What sort of things are you going to do? Are you prepared?

It can't happen to you right?

EMERGENCY PROCEDURES

I was flying enroute to Cedar Rapids, Iowa (KCID) on December 26th from Cambridge, Ohio (KCDI) with my wife and dog aboard. We could not make it through the weather direct to Cedar Rapids because a weather system with indicated convective activity had tracked northward across our flight path. We flew the RNAV Y 12 into Gary, Indiana (KGYY) and stopped for about 1.5 hours while the precipitation passed off to the North-East. We took on full fuel at Gary. Preflight inspection revealed that the tanks were indeed topped and the contents appeared to be 100LL and free of water contamination. I filed IFR to Cedar Rapids with a nearly direct flight because the Aviationweather.gov icing forecast tool revealed that a direct flight was possible between 3,000 and 10,000 foot altitudes.

After a normal start and run up, we departed Runway 12 at Gary at 13:29 CST on a heading of 280. Pressures and temperatures were all normal as indicated on an Electronics International MVP-50P engine analyzer. Shortly after rotation, I could hear a cyclic "clacking" sound that reminded me of the overspeed indication I've heard in turbine aircraft simulators. It was not terribly loud, and the engine was still developing full power. I assumed it was something like an anti-chafe strip that had come unglued and was smacking against the fuselage. This "clacking" continued throughout the climb and turn to heading.

All engine indications remained normal throughout the initial climb, and I had reduced power to 25" MP / 2,500 RPM then engaged autopilot. We climbed through a 1,000 foot thick layer with bases of around 600-700 feet AGL. As the climb continued, I leaned the engine for 1,375 degrees Fahrenheit EGT as normal. Just prior to reaching cruise altitude of 6,000 feet, the engine felt rough with a momentary decrease in RPM, then about a few seconds later, a complete loss of engine power.

I tried sweeping through the throttle control with no effect, going full rich, sweeping the mixture control closer to cutoff, then back to where it was. None of this had any effect on power. Sometime while doing this, I had disconnected the autopilot and pitched for 110 KIAS. Shortly thereafter, I turned on the electric fuel pump, saw indicated fuel pressure jump on the MVP display but smelled a very strong fuel smell. This also did not cause the engine to start developing any power. The fuel smell caused me to go ahead and shut down the electric pump and put the tank and mixture to cutoff. I guess I was thinking I was darn sure not going to go down in flames. Nothing seemed like it was going to bring the engine back anyway.

So at some point during all of this, I had managed to call up Chicago Approach and declare a MAYDAY. Yes, literally "Mayday," three times, followed by announcing the engine failure, and told Approach I was turning to the nearest airport, which appeared to be KIGQ (Lansing Municipal). I had Garmin Pilot pulled up on the Map page on my iPad, and it was literally the closest airport about 90 degrees left of course and proceeded at best glide, prop pulled to low RPM. At some point when I got to what appeared to be abeam the airport, I switched the iPad over to Synthetic Vision (SVS) page and could see the runway layout and the (thankfully flat) terrain. Chicago Approach offered up the runway information at KIGQ. I think I replied something about I was going to land on the first one I could see. They also offered the Gary, IN weather. Farther down into the descent, I queried about what was the field elevation at KIGQ.

I circled the perimeter of the airport, as I saw it in the SVS display, in a left-hand standard rate turn, at approximately 110 KIAS. I kept scanning between the SVS and out my left window, waiting to pop out of the layer. At what must have been the same 600 or 700 AGL I departed in, I saw a runway out the window, and it must have been Runway 18-36. The 18 approach end was in tight and was an impossible turn in the altitude remaining. Having broken out, I set the gear down, but kept flaps up. I looked farther out front and saw Runway 27 out in front, but little altitude remaining to turn on to it. Basically I was heading northbound and turned the airplane toward mid-field since there wasn't much to hit there.

Just prior to a nice clearing at mid-field (27-09) I saw a deep drainage ditch out in front and perpendicular to my path. I remember telling my wife to "Brace for impact." Somehow, by the grace of God, the airplane got in ground effect and managed to stay off long enough to clear that ditch.

We ended up in soft, but flat ground. I still had the airplane pointed at the runway when we touched, and kept the nose up in the roll out as best I could. Apparently when we reached the Runway 27 centerline I must have kicked the rudder to the left and lined the airplane up on the centerline for the rest of the rollout. When it stopped I tried to key on the #1 COMM, bottom antenna, and tell approach we were on the ground. Didn't get a reply, probably wasn't the best thing to be doing. I think at that point I looked over at the wife, said "evacuate the airplane." She was a bit confused about that at first, opened the door, while I grabbed the dog up in my arms and carried her (the dog) out.

4 minutes and 30 seconds from engine failure to touchdown.

Takeaways:

1) Reading crash reports on Beechtalk can save your life! I recall a similar A36 engine failure in IMC, New Jersey I think, where the pilot let ATC fly the airplane, didn't get anywhere near an airport, struck a house, and died. That liveATC recording was sad as hell and etched in my memory from months ago. There was discussion about whether to accept ATC vectors all over hell and back, try to fly an approach, or circle over an airport until you break out. If you turned straight for the airport, had the altitude, then that last one works. At least you'll end up over something flat and sparsely populated. Don't waste altitude.

2) Fancy avionics like Synthetic Vision can be worth every penny. I have a FlightStream 210 driving an iPad mini with Garmin Pilot. Remind me to send a thank you note to Garmin. That thing worked.

3) I was able to pull this off because the ceiling was >= 600 ft. The outcome could have been very different if I didn't have the time to find the field. Legal isn't necessarily safe. I have a new personal departure minimum.

As for myself, I'm a CFI, just short of 1,000 hours total time. I'm thankful I practice my spiral descents, 180 degree precision power off landings, and yell at my students to "just fly the damn airplane." There wasn't time for much else.

With permission from Mr. Matt Anker, 1970 Bonanza A36

I learned that danger is relative, and the
inexperience can be a magnifying glass.

— Charles A. Lindbergh

Emergency Procedure Basics

When you start USAF pilot training, one of the things that the instructors literally drill into your head is the following mantra regarding Emergency Procedures (EPs). We will refer to this henceforth as "the mantra." This phrase is practiced daily and is required to be quoted verbatim at the beginning of every "stand-up" emergency procedures quiz.

"Sir/Ma'am, I will maintain aircraft control, analyze the situation, take proper action, and land as soon as conditions permit."

I know it seems a bit cheesy, maybe even a bit simplistic, but you can quite literally apply that phrase, and those steps to every EP situation in any aircraft. At least that's the idea. Ask any current or former USAF pilot for the emergency procedures phrase, and I guarantee he or she will remember it.

The point of that phrase and why it is still important to USAF aircrew today is that it clearly defines what steps in order need to be taken to safely recover the aircraft. They must be done in that order, every time. Without maintaining aircraft control, one cannot even begin to analyze the situation or take actions. Once each step is accomplished, and continually updated, then and only then can the pilot move on to the next step in the sequence.

Please consider the above mantra for your training. It is quite literally the phrase that has been taught and used by tens of thousands of USAF pilots and crews for decades.

CAPs / Checklist

In the USAF community, all aircraft have checklists and Technical Order (T.O.) guidance. The pilot portion of these Technical Orders are also called the "dash 1" due to the naming convention for these aircraft publications. Much like every aircraft in the USAF inventory, the F-16 has mountains of publications and T.O.s. Everything from maintenance, to weapons loading, to pilot procedures are detailed in the Technical Orders. The F-16-1 (dash one) is the pilot's manual. The F-16-34 (dash thirty four) is weapons T.O.s. There are multitudes of other T.O.s for various other functions, all with a different numbering system. Simply put, an Air Force dash 1 is basically akin to the POH that you are already familiar with in your GA aircraft.

Within the dash 1, all aircraft have an Emergency Procedures section or chapter. In this section, various EPs are detailed and checklist guidance and procedures are outlined.

A few select EPs have what we call Critical Action Procedures, or CAPs. CAPs are written in boldface print and are sometimes referred to as "the boldface" as well. CAPs are required to be memorized. In my USAF experience, we filled out CAPs practice sheets (from memory of course) every month, and during initial training, young students were required to fill them out every week! Memorizing the CAPs was not terribly difficult for most pilots, but after filling out a CAPs sheet every month for multiple years as well as reciting CAPs on check rides, most pilots tended to be able to deliver them in their sleep. But that was the idea of course.

The original idea behind the CAPs was that some test pilot or safety board of experts, way-back-when, decided that certain emergency situations would require immediacy and need to be executed rapidly and accurately upon recognition of that particular EP situation. Because of the nature of the EP, there would *not* be time to delve into a checklist and take the time to read the actions required. The situation and these emergencies required immediate action.

In the F-16, items like a flameout, or airborne engine restart, or a fire during engine start and emergency ground egress are all CAPs. You'd better know how to do those things without reference to a checklist! Modern airline pilots and crews also use memory items or CAPs when flying the jumbos.

This is not to say that the checklist was tossed aside during these critical EPs. Most EPs are fairly in-depth, and you'd need that checklist to accomplish all tasks for a safe recovery. Additionally, during check rides, evaluators would ensure pilots and crews were always referencing the checklists. Failure to open the checklists and even reference it was a sure-fire way to bust your check ride and suffer bad marks on your "permanent flying record." Some EPs even have CAPs that are followed by extensive checklist procedures and decision matrices. The EP wasn't always over at the conclusion of the CAPs.

Personally, I enjoy the 'comfort' of the checklists and given a problem, anomaly or emergency, referencing the checklist always ensures for me that no key steps or items are missed. We were certainly trained to use the checklists. So please *please* do reference your checklists and have them ready and accessible in your cockpit.

But let's take all this one step further.

I propose that we develop a set of CAPs for *your* use, in *your* plane, in accordance with your POH. Your POH might already have some steps clearly outlined; you can start there and develop your own CAPs. Later in this chapter I will outline my engine failure CAPs for the Bonanza which can easily carry over to most GA piston singles.

Energy Management

Before we get too far into this EP debate and particularly the engine out scenarios for GA and Bonanza aircraft, let us take a brief look at some of the F-16 procedures, checklists and patterns as well as some energy management techniques…just for fun!

You might think that this stuff is really not very relevant to you and your single engine piston, and you might be right. The F-16 glides like the proverbial brick as they say, while your GA piston probably has a glide ratio that is far better. The Bonanza is typically 1.7/1,000 meaning it will glide 1.7 nm for every 1,000 feet of altitude. You already know that from our first chapter, and you might also realize that the F-16 glide parameters are not very close to this. Feel free to skim this section if you choose, however I am simply attempting to give a little background and take a snapshot of what the fighter pilots debate at the bar, and throw out a few terms and ideas that maybe you can apply to your training and knowledge. If you're still with me…here we go!

We can't have a fighter pilot style discussion of engine out procedures without first understanding energy (and energy management) as well as understanding this thing called a "wire." Let's go into it with a little more depth.

What is energy as far as the pilot is concerned? Energy or *energy state* is a reference to a summative collection of potential and kinetic energy of the aircraft. Altitude and airspeed to put it simply. An SR-71 at 80,000 feet MSL going Mach 3 has tremendous energy. A single engine piston at pattern altitudes and airspeeds has far lower energy than our SR-71. But energy is relative right? Huh? Hold on, we'll get to that in a minute.

When it comes to energy states, different aircraft can have *similar* energy states but be in *different* parts of the sky. For example, an aircraft can have high airspeed but low altitude, an F-16 on a 500 KIAS low-level for instance. A similar *energy state* might be that same F-16 up at 20,000 feet but going very slowly. Even though the aircraft have opposite altitudes and airspeeds, each could conceivably have similar (or the same) energy states. The low-level F-16 could trade that airspeed for altitude and 'pop-up' to 10,000 feet in a just a few seconds. Conversely, the slow F-16 at 20,000 feet could trade in his altitude for airspeed by diving to 10,000 feet and regaining airspeed. Don't get too caught up in the numbers, I know I promised no math, but the concepts and ideas are important to understand for the tactical pilot as well as the pilot faced with an engine out situation.

After one starts to understand energy states, energy management and *precision* energy management becomes easy.

But we also said that energy was relative. This is true. It is relative, but only when compared to something else. Sure, the SR-71 in the stratosphere has tremendous energy as compared to the single engine Bonanza in the pattern. That is obvious. But let's compare those energy states not against each airplane or each other, but in something we, as single engine pilots would care about…landing engine out for instance!

Each of these energy states in the above scenario can and should be compared to something. In this case, we'd like to compare the energy states of each airplane to a point on the earth. For now, let's have that point on earth be "brick one" or "the numbers" on an imaginary runway. You could also call it our landing point. Still with me?

The SR-71 (yes, I know it has two engines) has the aforementioned massive energy state right? But what if he's 800 miles from a suitable landing surface? Is he high or low on energy relative to that landing point? Low of course! No matter what he does, if he becomes a glider he will not be able to glide to a safe touchdown at the landing point, regardless of his speed and altitude.

Now take the Bonanza in the pattern again. He has much lower energy overall as we stated, but for him, he just might be able to make a glide to the landing spot if he lost his engine. It depends on the Bonanza's airspeed and altitude at the time he begins his glide, his flightpath, his subsequent ground path, and how the aircraft is situated relative to that point on the ground.

Okay, enough about energy. I hope you understand what I'm getting at is that energy is comprised of some formula, or combination of altitude and airspeed. Your job is to trade both of those in to make a successful touchdown, at your desired point on the earth, safely.

The Wire

So what is this wire thing? Let's take a closer look at that. I know we also mentioned this a little in the Glide Basics chapter, but let's dig a touch deeper and also refresh on the concept.

Basically, a wire in fighter terminology is a glide path. A simple three degree ILS could be said to have a three degree "wire." We use multiple glide paths in the F-16 to describe multiple flying events. A 30 degree nose low diving weapons delivery will have a 30 degree wire, where as a stabilized visual approach to the runway in the F-16 is typically flown on a 2.5 degree glide path or 2.5 degree wire. So the wire is really just a synonymous term for a glide path. And your aircraft can either be physically above or below the wire (when it comes to energy state). Just like on a glideslope to an ILS approach.

Think of the wire as an actual wire, or string, or ribbon with one end tied to a stake at the landing point and the other end traveling skyward at 10 or 20, or 30 degrees, whatever.

For this book I attempted to obtain approval to use some of the F-16 dash 1 technical manual pictures and drawings. Unfortunately, due to their sensitivity, I was denied the use of these illustrations. (Hint: some are available in the interwebs if you dig around). Below in figure 7 is a rough diagram of what the F-16 SFO illustration looks like (sorry, I'm no artist). The *key distinction* I'd like you to take from this sketch is noting the wire or line in the sky the aircraft is following.

We'll take a closer look at this in a few more pages, however have a look at the turning glide line or "ribbon" depicting the F-16s airborne path during the SFO. Note how it curves and circles, eventually lining up with a final approach portion and touchdown on the runway. This curved path through the air is also a wire! The wire doesn't have to necessarily be straight or aligned with the runway.

A wire can also be that imaginary line or ribbon in the sky that might diverge in path, or turn…but it never varies in descent degrees or angle. Just like an ILS never varies its glide-slope angle. Got it?

F-16 Overhead SFO Drawing
Figure 7

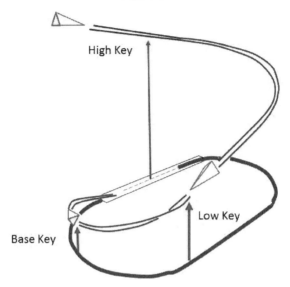

During weapons attack passes, ILS approaches or the basic SFO practice EP glide maneuver in the F-16, we commonly assess our energy state relative to the wire. Say I wanted an eight degree wire on a particular day during some SFO practice. Or to put it a better way, say that during a practice SFO glide my particular weight and CG *determined for me* that an eight degree wire would be needed for me to glide to the touchdown spot. Once I knew this, I could then adjust my energy state and nose-low glide angle to get on that eight degree wire. We'll look at how we can easily see that eight degree wire in the cockpit in a second, but for now, understand that the gliding performance of your airplane is a set sink rate (or glide ratio) for a given airspeed. As mentioned earlier, there is also one particular AoA that coincides with best glide airspeed too.

What you can affect is the placement of your airplane on that wire by adjusting either airspeed or altitude. Effectively trading either (or both) in for a change to hopefully arrive on the wire at the best glide airspeed and allow for a nice touchdown on the landing surface.

The Ribbon In the Sky

How does one trade energy in an airplane? How do you go from high altitude to a lower altitude? Maybe you find yourself high or steep on the wire or glide path. It's of course quite simple right? You lower the nose. Just like your CFI on your first lesson taught you. Easy huh? But wait a minute. There are a few things to understand here, and one needs to understand the consequences of trading energy.

Trading in energy for a lower energy state is critical to your safe engine out recovery. Like we mentioned earlier, you pretty much will (hopefully) be in a position and an energy state to trade or swap high energy for lower energy to capture the wire. If you are below the wire and low on energy already when faced with a glide, there is not much you can do to gain energy and recapture the wire. For that reason we will not detail it much in this writing. Cutting the corner or proceeding directly to the point of intended landing is about the only thing you can do to regain any energy, aside from making the airplane cleaner and less draggy.

Therefore losing energy and trading it in for a lower position closer to the wire is the most common technique we practice. What are a few common methods to lose energy?

Drag. Adding drag is the biggest way in which you can lose energy. Two excellent techniques to lose energy and add drag are: lower the gear, or push the propeller lever forward to gain a windmilling propeller. However, both of those techniques are fairly aggressive and will take energy away from you quickly and consistently throughout the remainder of the profile. These techniques may not be available for some fixed gear aircraft as well. For those reasons, I do not recommend blindly dropping the gear or returning the prop forward.

What I prefer to do, is to take small nibbles out of my energy situation, and then assess the outcome. One of my favorite tricks is a simple slip. It works well. Another great technique is to *get farther away* from the landing surface. Remember our SR-71 discussion? He was so far from the field that he was low on energy. You can do the same, very easily. A quick *fade* away from the runway and back, or an extension on the overhead SFO will reduce energy nicely without giving up or spoiling any stable pitch and airspeed settings that you have worked on so hard to perfect. Extensions and turns away from the landing surface also work well in IMC FO situations as you are looking to minimize turning in the weather and possible Spatial Disorientation problems. S-Turns work well to lose energy as well when VMC.

All in all, what you are looking to do is to make the line you are flying, that ribbon in the sky...longer. If you can stretch out that ribbon from start to finish, you are increasing your *time* in the glide and thusly lowering your energy state overall. But the trick is to not lose too much energy and go below the wire. This "ribbon in the sky" thought process is an excellent way to lose energy in the FO/SFO pattern and it won't affect your airspeed, glide ratio, or sink rate.

When do we trade in energy, and how do you manage your energy during the glide? The time to trade in energy is up high, early in the profile. You need to stay above the wire at all times, and then carefully work your way down to the wire by cautiously planned energy depleting maneuvers as you execute the glide to the runway or landing surface. To lose energy, take small bites. If you are above the wire and high on energy, do not do an aggressive energy depleting maneuver as you do not want to go below the wire accidentally. "Nibble" your way down to the wire slowly throughout the glide profile, and assess. As Mr. Anker stated above "don't waste altitude."

It is permissible to briefly go below the wire if you have the energy to come back up to the wire AND retain that target airspeed. But going below the wire, while low on energy, or with anything less than target airspeed is a sure way to end up crashing short.

By now, I hope you understand the relationship of energy and energy management a little better. If you are high, you just lower the nose to get lower, but the tradeoff is increased airspeed. Conversely, if you are low, you can climb, but this slows you down. And all of this energy trading is of course *relative* to the wire, which is the *key* as it leads you to the landing spot.

You have to think of the wire and your position relative to it three-dimensionally. If you are low on the glide path during an engine out situation, and you choose to climb back up to the wire, you have chosen to trade some airspeed energy for some altitude energy. This might help you regain the wire and fix the glide path situation, but in that tradeoff, you have sacrificed airspeed and new problems emerge (like a deep sink rate or maybe even a stall).

What I want you to recognize, and the way in which fighter pilots train to the engine out situation is realizing that airspeed (and glidepath/wire) are fixed, locked or "frozen." Your airspeed in the glide is essentially set in stone. Your glide ratio or wire is also set in stone by your aircraft designers. It's the same in the Bonanza or any other single engine airplane. The engineers have figured out what the best glide speed is, and your job as the pilot is to fly that airspeed during the glide.

With those two variables fixed (the wire and the glide speed), all you can do is control your placement and position of your aircraft on that wire. The ribbon.

At the end of it all, once you positively know you have the landing spot made, then and only then is it recommended to trade in all excess energy to arrive on the wire and finish the landing.

Don't worry too much yet on how we'll visually see the wire in our piston single engine birds. We'll cover that in more depth shortly. For now, I want you to understand the general concept of the wire and energy trading and energy states, relative to the wire.

F-16 CAPs

Let's take a look at the F-16 CAPs (General Electric engine) for an engine loss or air start inflight. Interestingly, the dash 1 for the F-16 does not have any procedures for *engine loss in flight,* technically speaking. The CAPs and procedures are for *restarting* the engine (technically called an Air Start). These are designed to possibly to save an engine that is coughing, sputtering or has flamed out. Those steps, from the F-16 dash 1 are as follows:

Engine - SEC then PRI

Airspeed - As Required (250 KIAS or Max range or endurance airspeed)

JFS - Start 2 (below 20,000 ft and 400 KIAS)

To break it down, engine SEC then PRI refers to placing the engine in more of a manual mode versus a computerized mode that we normally operate in. In the computer mode, the computer controls the engine inlet blades and a nozzle schedule, as well as fuel metering and other engine management items. This computer driven engine scheduling is known as the Primary, or PRI setting. This apparently has been the cause of some past engine failures and resetting the engine computer or flying in SEC has saved a few engines (and F-16s).

The airspeed part in step two generally requires at least 250 KIAS or better. For one, this speed preserves windmilling RPM of the engine which aids in restarting the engine, and two, it can possibly blow out any flame, fire or air turbulence in the engine duct.

The JFS is the Jet Fuel Starter. Basically it's the starter for the motor, and once you are below the maximum altitudes and airspeeds for it to operate, that last step of the CAPs is basically akin to 'turning the ignition key.'

It's also worthy of note that there are also CAPs in front of air start CAPs above if you were considered in the low altitude environment. A zoom (fast climb) and stores jettison were the CAPs for that flight regime, followed by the above restart/

air start CAPs. Following the air start CAPs, the dash 1 has at least four more subsequent important steps to accomplish if a relight doesn't occur, but those are not considered CAPs. Fighter pilots refer to these "important" steps jokingly as the "non-CAP CAPs." They are incredibly important and you'd probably want them committed to memory because if your air start was failing, I doubt you'd have time to pull out the checklist in an F-16 and begin to thumb through its pages.

The particulars of those steps are not specific to this discussion or book; however they illustrate a good point that there are often many steps required in the successful completion of an emergency checklist, and some are required to be memorized and recalled under extreme duress.

So to sum up the F-16 CAPs for air start in our above example, we've noted that they are technically not engine failure CAPs, but are instead engine restart CAPs and procedures. Some steps are critical and must happen fast after the decision is made to execute them, and others, while important, can be done later if the restart fails or struggles.

F-16 Overhead SFO

The F-16 dash 1 describes various altitudes required at different points around the overhead SFO/FO pattern. In the F-16 the entry altitudes could change significantly based on gross weight. This is not the case so much with your light single engine GA bird, right? Remember our earlier lesson about glide ratios and weight?

However, in the F-16, with potentially thousands of pounds of fuel and weapons we would commonly have dramatic changes in our best glide speeds and actual glide ratio. Shortly after takeoff at maximum gross weight of over 37,000 pounds, the fuel weight alone could vary by as much 12,000 pounds typically. That's basically one-third of the weight of the aircraft in fuel alone. Now add stores, tanks and bombs and you could really have a wide range of landing speeds and altitude "windows" at the various key positions. By the way, AoA was a huge help in these circumstances. We will cover that in a later section, but knowing the best glide AoA regardless of these massive weight and speed differences made all the difference in the Viper. Your 3,400 pound Bonanza only carries 14 percent of its maximum weight in fuel, so it's a little less dramatic.

Let's take a closer look at the overhead SFO for the F-16. Refer back to figure 7 for a rough sketch. The overhead SFO was designed as a training maneuver only. It was built for repeated SFO practice, energy management practice, and pattern sequencing and procedures so USAF controllers have some kind of idea what the pilot is doing and can sequence traffic appropriately. That's not to say that the overhead SFO isn't useful for an actual FO, but generally, it's accepted that the overhead SFO is not viable for a real-world FO unless you happen to be exactly over the field at the appropriate altitude when your engine quit. Generally F-16 pilots prefer a straight-in FO for real-world planning and engine out execution, however again, the overhead SFO was good for repetitive practice and sight picture development. I'd recommend for your training, that you begin with an overhead SFO engine out procedure, and I'll show you more of how to do that in the next chapter.

The specifics of the F-16 SFO were that you would approach High Key at 7-10 thousand feet above the field depending on weight. High Key is directly above the point of intended landing. We are also taught to aim for the first third of the runway as an initial aimpoint. Once arriving at High Key, you configure for the SFO by setting power to idle, extending partial speed brakes, and dropping the gear (if desired) and pitching down to a nose low attitude that would hold the best glide speed/AoA you wanted. Additionally, rolling into 50-55 degrees of bank was desired as well to set up for the downwind, and you would attempt to have one nautical mile spacing from the runway for your final downwind spacing.

Following the downwind you would arrive at Low Key. The Low Key position technically varies dependent on wind and weights, but the one nautical mile offset from the runway would always be the spacing goal. After a fair bit of practice doing SFOs, the Low Key position would become a point in space that you could get a feel for based upon sight picture alone. If you are a little high on energy, you can extend past Low Key for a few seconds to shave off some energy and lower yourself on the wire. If the opposite was true and you find yourself low on energy approaching Low Key, then an immediate turn in toward the runway would be required, to not go below the wire. The bottom line is that the Low Key position was somewhat variable.

Optimally, you would arrive at Base Key about 1 1/4 nm from the numbers and 2,000+ feet above the ground. Remember, this whole time, during this maneuver, you are aiming for the first third of the runway. If you've done things correctly, you will typically notice that at Base Key you will be slightly high on altitude. This is desirable as it's easy to lose energy and airspeed in an F-16, especially if you haven't lowered the gear by this point. On short final, the dash 1 calls for a transition to a "nose-even-lower" sight picture to both increase airspeed and move the desired touchdown point closer to the near side of the runway. This was the F-16 technique, and care must be exercised to not get too low and slow and possibly touchdown short of the prepared surface! This was also known as our "cashing it in" technique. Like we discussed above, we only cashed in all that extra energy once we positively knew that we had the landing surface made. Only then was it safe to transition to an aim point at "brick one" in an attempt to use all available runway.

So there you have it! A quick and basic rundown of the Viper overhead SFO. I'm sure you have some questions. Please realize that I am not trying to train you on how to fly an F-16 SFO or FO via this writing. Instead I am illustrating some of the basics of the military procedures and their differences to the GA procedures, and also what standard I believe the GA pilot should be training to. I will break down this style of SFO for us GA pilots in a future section.

Please also realize that these military procedures have been tried and tested for decades in the F-16 and other military single engine aircraft with similar maneuvers since the Cold War era. This modern F-16 SFO pattern is nearly identical to "your father's SFO."

I am by no means saying that these methods are "the best" or are the only way to go. But I would like you, the reader and pilot of your single engine beast, to better understand what highly refined and complete procedures for engine out patterns actually look like, and the above brief description was a start, and a quick look into the military SFO pattern.

F-16 Straight-In SFO

What does a straight-in SFO / FO for the F-16 look like? It's really quite simple. Looking at figure 8 below for a quick depiction sketch, note that there are certain defined points along an extended centerline to the runway. Specifically, Points A and B, and Area C. We will define these points in more depth in a later section, but here, I'd like you to simply have a basic understanding of the straight-in SFO. You are either above or below the wire at those points. If you are high, you need to complete some kind of energy depleting maneuver to regain the wire. If you are low, you might not make the field unless you could conserve energy and somehow regain energy (leave the gear up, stores jettison, etc.) relative to the wire. And if you are really low, there's always the ejection seat.

The straight-in SFO is generally quite simple, but merits practice. It was from this straight-in SFO that most (if not all) F-16 pilots anticipated how their real-world engine loss scenario would successfully be flow. We didn't spend much time flying the F-16 above the airfield, the bad guys were not generally found there, so the straight-in FO procedure was predicted to be the best everyday option.

We will delve into the straight-in SFO heavily, in the Training and Practice chapter.

F-16 Straight-In SFO Drawing
Figure 8

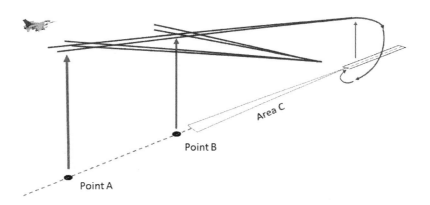

Area C

Point B

Point A

Finding Your Wire

How does one know what glide path or wire one is actually on? In the F-16 it was pretty simple. Figure 9 shows an example HUD and it's markings.

Basic HUD Example

Figure 9

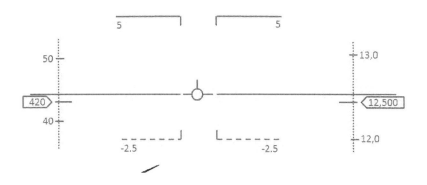

We typically had the convenience of a HUD, which over-laid pitch ladders on the environment in front of the pilot. When airborne, if the end of a runway was near the -5 (negative five) degree pitch ladder, well then the aircraft was five degrees above the runway, or would have to fly a 5 degrees descent in order to make it to that point. A five wire would be required to make it to the runway. Pretty simple, right?

In the above figure 9 graphic you can see a makeshift airfield in the distance that sits in the lower left portion of the HUD. Interpolation tells us that this airfield is about 3 to 4 degrees below the horizon. Knowing I need about an eight wire in the Viper for an engine out glide, if I lose the engine at that moment, I'm pretty certain that I could not make that field.

Even if the point of intended landing is outside (left or right) of the HUD, one could still visually transcribe that point over to the HUD and get a feel for how many degrees below the horizon that point is. See figure 10 for an example.

Cockpit View SFO
Figure 10

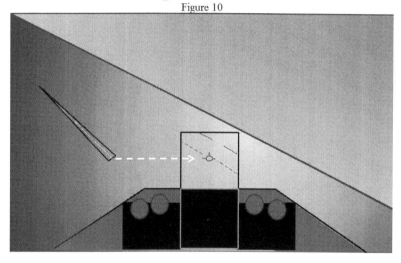

In this example the pilot of an F-16 in the Base Key to Final position can start to see that "brick one" is horizontally on the notional -10 (negative ten) degree pitch ladder and quickly ascertain an energy state reference and wire relationship for the aircraft.

Additionally, we have a Flight Path Marker (FPM). The FPM is an inertially derived (INS and air data system) symbol of where the aircraft is going and looks like a little circle with wings and a vertical tail. The significance of the FPM is in its relationship to AoA. Remember, the airplane is not always going to a magical point straight off the longitudinal line, or nose of the aircraft, but quite often to a place somewhere *below* the nose of course. The FPM helps the pilot see that relationship and adjust accordingly. With a FMP, one can "see" where the aircraft is truly going. Some of today's Synthetic Vision technology in GA is beginning to incorporate a FPM and pitch ladders.

You can get a feel for this effect in your single engine piston during slow flight. If doing slow flight correctly, you will be in level flight, yet your nose will be pointed skyward. Always remember that aircraft flightpath and where the nose is pointed are two separate things.

Finding the wire in a GA single engine aircraft is a little more difficult, and in some cases total guesswork. No, your pitch reference in your ADI is *NOT* the wire. Think back to your ILS known pitch and power settings. I'm betting that while flying a three degree ILS, your aircraft pitch attitude is closer to level to one degree nose low, or thereabouts. So the ADI wont help you find your wire.

Unfortunately, most GA singles do not have SVT game changing technology and the subsequent FPM to show flight path. Honestly, SVT is not that big of a deal when VMC. During 90% of overhead SFO practice in the F-16, the landing environment is nowhere near the HUD. It is below your shoulder or under your butt, and the fancy technology in the HUD is practically useless. After doing quite a few SFOs, we were pretty good at visually performing the maneuver and just visualizing the curved spiral wire, just like you do now in your aircraft in the final turn for a normal landing.

Without landing aids and VASIs and the like, I bet after some practice at your local field that you have become pretty good at visualizing the normal landing 'sight picture' in your aircraft. You didn't know it, but you were learning a skill that will be hugely valuable to your engine out practice, and you were unknowingly finding a two or three degree wire at the same time. Good work!

Bottom line: actually "seeing" the no kidding wire in your aircraft (without SVT and a FPM) is going to be impossible. But understanding the concept of that glide path and visualizing it is the next advanced tactic and skill you will need to hone.

Now you will need to develop a feel for the six degree wire and a sight-picture. More on that soon.

Bonanza Engine Out Procedures

NOTE: *Below I will describe some changes and suggestions to manufacturer's recommended guidance and checklist guidance. The user of these suggested procedures uses them at their own risk. Failure to use and follow manufacture guidance is at the discretion of the PIC. I will not be held responsible. Got it!?*

In this section we are going to take a look at the Bonanza, and its engine out checklists, procedures and recommendations. We'll also discuss those procedures and attempt to lay out some universal CAPs for Bonanza pilots (and certainly for pilots of other single engine aircraft as well). We will talk about a concept called "securing the engine" and then get into the actual nitty gritty of landing the Bonanza from a glide and some thoughts on when or if you should use the gear and or flaps.

I'll never forget one of my old CFIs way back when I was first getting my Private Pilot's license, Mr. O'Connor. He use to always, always, always say, "If your engine fails, the first thing you do is switch tanks!" I'll never forget it, and I can picture Mr. O'Connor now, sitting in the right seat of the little Cherokee 140 we trained in, somewhere over eastern Oklahoma. He used to say this to me all the time, and pretty much on every lesson. I don't think he ever referenced the checklist, he certainly never taught me to open one up and look into it given a failure or emergency. For all I ever knew, these were his version of the CAPs, and that was it. We practiced it many times until the motion and actions became ingrained in my (knuckle) head.

Then one night, many years later, in October 1996, I was flying the same little Cherokee. I was coming back from visiting friends up in Wichita, Kansas and was returning to Oklahoma. For some reason I was flying home at night, but it was clear across the plains. My logbook notes heavy headwinds on the flight home.

I'll never forget the return leg of that trip. I had calculated that I had about an hour of fuel remaining at my destination when I took off from Wichita, this was no problem I assumed. But man those headwinds were fierce!

I was nearing the northwest corner of Oklahoma City, headed for my home field of Shawnee that was ten to fifteen Cherokee 140 minutes due east of OKC. I could begin to make out the lights of the big city and the beacon and air-field lights for Wiley Post airfield which lay on the northwest edge of Oklahoma City. Just then the engine sputtered and stopped! Holy shit! I thought, as I instinctively reached down and switched the tank selector to the other side. The engine coughed and came back to life nicely. I had just run a tank dry, and I wasn't prepared for it.

After some heavy breathing and wide-eyed instrument scanning, I was comfortable that everything was okay, but my heart was still racing. Now second guessing my fuel computa-tions and the not-so accurate leaning technique of "lean to the roughness" and then add two twists to the mixture knob, I was really uncertain of my remaining fuel state. The goofy Piper fuel gauges bounced around in the light bumps at altitude. Sure enough the right tank indicated empty, and the left tank that I was now flying off of, was showing pretty low as well. Do I trust my fuel 'guessing' and fuel burn guesstimates? That was the question looming in my head.

Nope. I elected to begin a descent and put her down at the familiar field of Wiley Post in the dark. I had been there many times in the past for the then $50 hamburger, or to see Dr. Brent Heisy's P-51 "Miss America" that was almost always available to gawk at.

I'll never forget the queasy and uneasy feeling of descending in the dark, uncertain of my *exact* fuel state (thanks Piper fuel needles and nonexistent fuel flow gauges). I was just hoping the engine didn't quit on me.

It didn't and boy did I feel relieved to get on the ground and taxi into the FBO after scaring myself quite adequately.

The moral of the story (besides doing better fuel calculations and monitoring of fuel flow), is that if the engine quits or sputters, the first step of your CAPs should be to switch tanks Why? Because the majority of accidents related to engine failures from fuel mismanagement are staggering and quite common.

The 2011 Nall Report shows us that in the Flight Planning and Decision-Making category of accidents, fuel mismanagement statistics are again on the rise even as the number of fixed-wing accidents have declined. "Fuel mismanagement caused just over 6% of the [total] accidents in 2008, but almost 8% in 2011." Failures to determine the amount of fuel required or on board and enroute accounted for 47% of accidents in this category and errors in operating the aircraft's fuel system comprised another 45% of accidents. So in the Flight Planning and

Decision-Making category, *nearly all* of the accidents that year were fuel and fuel delivery related. That is a staggering statistic! Other year's statistics are not much different.

With that in mind, let's now take a look at some checklists. Figure 11 contains an excerpt from the V35/V35A/V35B (1966-1976) POH. Note a couple interesting checklists on the first half of the page. We see a ROUGH RUNNING ENGINE checklist and a LOSS OF ENGINE POWER checklist. If we read the ROUGH RUNNING ENGINE checklist we see some pretty logical steps. Mixture rich then lean (also known as the mixture sweep), magnetos (mags) left right and both, and of course in the Bonanza, alternate air T-handle pull and release.

Figure 11

BEECHCRAFT Bonanza   Section III
V35, V35A & V35B thru D-9947 Emergency Procedures

ENGINE DISCREPANCY CHECKS

CONDITION: ROUGH RUNNING ENGINE

1. Mixture - FULL RICH, then LEAN as required
2. Magneto/Start Switch - CHECK LEFT and RIGHT, then BOTH
3. Alternate Air T-handle - PULL AND RELEASE

CONDITION: LOSS OF ENGINE POWER

1. Fuel Flow Gage - CHECK

If fuel flow is abnormally low:
    a. Mixture - FULL RICH
    b. Auxiliary Fuel Pump - ON (Lean as required)
    c. Auxiliary Fuel Pump - OFF if performance does not improve in a few moments

2. Fuel Quantity Indicator - CHECK for fuel supply in tank being used
3. Alternate Air T-handle - PULL AND RELEASE

If tank being used is empty:
Fuel Tank Selector Valve - SELECT OTHER FUEL TANK (feel for detent and check visually)

AIR START PROCEDURE

    a. Fuel Selector Valve - SELECT TANK MORE NEARLY FULL (check to feel detent)
    b. Throttle - RETARD
    c. Mixture - FULL RICH
    d. Auxiliary Fuel Pump - ON until power is regained, then OFF. (Leave on if engine driven fuel pump is inoperative.)
    e. Throttle - ADVANCE to desired power
    f. Mixture - LEAN as required

January 1982   3-5

All of these checklist items seem pretty straightforward to any piston engine that might be running roughly. Adjust the mixture in case the fuel delivery or air density is the culprit, checking the ignition system via the mag switch to see if one mag is better or worse than the other, and lastly, pulling the alternate air door which in the Bonanza, allows for full (unfiltered) air to enter the intake manifold by bypassing the air filter element that sits in the nose bowl. Sometimes, these air filters get clogged or impacted with ice, which will make the engine gasp and wheeze due to too little air for combustion.

As you know, it takes three things to make an engine run. Fuel, air, and spark as they say. If any one of these fails, you no longer have a running engine. Looking at the ROUGH RUNNING ENGINE checklist, it should be obvious as to what and why we have those three steps. Fuel, air, and spark, of course!

Next let's take a look at the subsequent checklist, LOSS OF ENGINE POWER. Note that step one is to check the fuel flow gage [gauge]. Please understand that we are not checking the fuel *quantity* gauge here, but instead we are examining the fuel flow. If fuel flow is low, there is something preventing fuel from reaching the engine.

The following steps in the checklist do a substantial job of troubleshooting this situation when you do find low fuel flow. Step one is to go full rich on the mixture. This makes sense right…maybe we just messed up the mixture setting for the regime of flight we are currently in. The second step is to turn the Aux fuel pump on, and then off "in a few moments" if the conditions do not improve. This step is present because sometimes the engine driven fuel pump, which automatically delivers fuel to the engine when it is turning, can sometimes fail or even become disconnected from the engine crankshaft. If this fails, there is no way that fuel can be delivered to the engine, except by the aux boost pump. All of the above steps fall under the "check fuel flow" step.

After that, note that the checklist step two is to now check for fuel quantity, and then also to pull the alternate air T-handle in step three.

Of note, the Bonanza A36 checklists (not included in this book) add the Aux fuel pump step into the checklist for a rough running engine, followed by the above V35 checklist steps of adjusting mixture, checking the magnetos, and pulling the alternate air T-handle. For some reason the A36 checklist does not contain a loss of engine power checklist. But I can see why Beech may have removed that checklist. Effectively, one can just add the aux fuel pump step to the rough running engine checklist (which again, helps our fuel, air, and spark combustion triangle) and by doing so very easily solves both engine discrepancy situations.

I happen to like both of these above checklists. Do you see the way in which each checklist works the problem in order of most likely failure to the lowest probability of failure? I think these checklists are actually quite smart and they should also apply very nicely to just about any single engine piston airplane. Sure, some aircraft have carburetors or different aux and boost pumps, but they all need fuel, air, and spark to fly. And faced with any sort of engine problem, troubleshooting the fuel, air, and spark delivery methods and systems in your plane will be a fantastic place to start.

Lastly, both the V35 and the A36 in fact have nicely organized engine failure checklists. The V35 technically has an air start checklist (like the F-16!), and that checklist is nearly identical to the A36 ENGINE FAILURE checklist but with a couple minor differences. Let's have a look.

Figure 12 shows the V35 engine failure checklist. There is a section for engine failure during takeoff ground roll, and one for after liftoff and in flight. We will focus on the after liftoff and in flight checklist as the ground roll engine failure checklist is basically just the steps to secure the engine and abort the takeoff.

The V35 steps for airborne engine failure inflight are as follows (slightly abbreviated):

1. Fuel Selector - Select other tank
2. Aux fuel pump - On
3. Mixture - Full rich, then lean
4. Magnetos - Check left, right, both
5. Alternate air T-handle - Pull and release

Figure 12

Section III   **BEECHCRAFT Bonanza**
Emergency Procedures V35, V35A & V35B thru D-9947

ENGINE FAILURE

DURING TAKE-OFF GROUND ROLL

1. Throttle - CLOSED
2. Braking - MAXIMUM
3. Fuel Selector Valve - OFF
4. Battery and Alternator Switches - OFF

AFTER LIFTOFF AND IN FLIGHT

Landing straight ahead is usually advisable. If sufficient altitude is available for maneuvering, accomplish the following:

1. Fuel Selector Valve - SELECT OTHER TANK (Check to feel detent)
2. Auxiliary Fuel Pump - ON
3. Mixture - FULL RICH, then LEAN as required
4. Magnetos - CHECK LEFT and RIGHT, then BOTH
5. Alternate Air T-handle - PULL AND RELEASE

NOTE

The most probable cause of engine failure would be loss of fuel flow, improper functioning of the ignition system or blockage of the induction system.

If No Restart

1. Select most favorable landing site.
2. See EMERGENCY LANDING procedure.
3. The use of landing gear is dependent on the terrain where landing must be made.

3-4   **January 1982**

The steps for the A36 engine failure are virtually identical except that the A36 checklist gives a glide airspeed to follow in the first step and omits the alternate air T-handle step until a subsequent checklist section called "if no restart." The

A36 checklist also reorders the steps slightly from the above V35 checklist.

Careful examination of the V35 engine failure checklist shows that the first three steps are fuel and fuel-delivery related! After that, the checklist tells the pilot to deal with the spark part of the system, followed by the air intake portion of the combustion triangle.

Personally, I like this arrangement. It seems to me that most engine failure scenarios would be fuel or fuel delivery related like our above statistics suggest, followed by the redundant twin magneto ignition system that we all fly with, and then lastly the quite low probability that no air is reaching the cylinders. I like that this checklist deals with the higher probability stuff first, and then goes down the list of ever decreasing likely failure culprits.

In the A36 checklist, the step for magnetos has been updated from the older V35 checklists. They are not telling the pilot to spend a bunch of time with his/her engine failing to turn the key and try the magnetos in various settings. Simply, the A36 magneto step is to *visually* verify that the ignition is still in BOTH. No key turning is occurring as in the V35 checklists. The remaining A36 steps are also all fuel and fuel delivery related. Nice!

The A36 checklist assumes that just by accomplishing the three fuel steps and visually checking the mags in BOTH that the engine will restart. Maybe the Beechcraft people have read the same statistics listed above as well. This checklist assumes a restart will occur, but only if it doesn't restart, will you proceed on to the follow-on checklist of turning off the aux fuel pump (in case the engine has too much fuel), going full rich on the mixture and then checking the mags in different settings. In your A36 after all of this, you will also pull the alternate air T-handle. Interesting.

Additionally, I also love the little note in the old V35 checklist at the bottom of the Engine Failure checklists. It states: "The most probable cause of engine failure would be loss of fuel flow, improper functioning of the ignition system or blockage of the induction system." Thanks Mr. Beech! Wow, there you have it, a clear description of why the engine would fail, one of the three required parts of the ignition triangle! Fuel, air, or spark. Pretty funny in my opinion. I love the old manuals and POHs.

So let's sum up all of this Bonanza checklist stuff. The V35 and the A36 Bonanza checklists give us some pretty darn good steps to follow in the event of an engine loss or even just engine troubleshooting inflight. Each are slightly different, but each generally troubleshoots the aircraft systems in order of what typically are the highest to lowest probable anomalies based on statistics. A smart structure if you ask me.

Now, let's take that knowledge and apply some smartness and pilot tactical-ness to it all and come up with a universal Bonanza (and quite possibly all of GA as well) checklist to commit to memory, and to follow, in the event you suffer from an engine loss inflight.

Bonanza CAPs (B-CAPs)

As always, manufacturer and POH guidance is paramount. That being said, I am recommending that you institute the following CAPs for your Bonanza, or possibly for your single engine GA piston. Regardless of what you fly, I am going to call them the B-CAPs, or Bonanza CAPs. Pronounced "Bee-Caps." For readers and adopters of this book, the B-CAPs will be the new industry standard.

These B-CAPs are merely recommendations; you can feel free to make your own or modify these to suit your needs. I ask that you commit them to memory, practice them on paper (maybe on the first of the month like we did in the USAF), and practice them in your airplane at one G and zero knots, as well as possibly in the air too by touching the controls in the correct order. Use them, but always follow POH guidance as well please.

Without further ado, below are the new B-CAPs for the Bonanza engine out, engine failure or engine sputter.

1. Glide - ESTABLISH
2. Fuel Selector - SELECT OTHER TANK

3. Aux fuel pump - ON
4. Mixture - SWEEP
5. Magnetos - VISUALLY CHECK BOTH

If no restart:
1. Aux Fuel Pump - OFF
2. Mixture - RICH
3. Magnetos - CHECK LEFT, RIGHT, BOTH
4. Alternate Air T-handle - PULL AND RELEASE

Sounds like a lot, right? Nine steps! Well much like the V35 and A36 checklists, you hopefully just have to do the first five steps. Hopefully. I am also prioritizing the first three steps (after Glide - ESTABLISH) to the fuel-related things. I also believe that fuel delivery (if there are no catastrophic engine mechanical breakdowns) will be the culprit. That is why I put those steps first. I also believe that the mags will gener-ally always be in BOTH (if you did your before takeoff checks correctly). That is why I suggest step five is like the A36 pro-cedures, to just visually check the mags. Assuming they were indeed found to be incorrect during step five and set to just Left or Right, it would be appropriate at this time in the B-CAPs to correct them and set the mags to BOTH.

The last four steps after "if no restart" I am also consider-ing B-CAPs (yes, this is a long CAPs checklist), but you could think of them as non-CAP CAPs like we discussed above, if you choose. Either way, I think these are some excellent steps combined from the V35 and A36 and you will want them committed to memory for when the first set of CAPs are not achieving a restart.

I'll say it again here: You have manufacturer's recommended guidance and checklists in your POH. You need to use and follow that guidance for your airplane, always. If you want to think of the above B-CAPs as memory joggers or steps to do before or after you run the paper checklists, then that would also be acceptable. I am humbly recommending some smart steps that you can use, but they do not *fully replace* the steps in your aircraft's POH.

After the B-CAPs / Securing the Engine

So now what? You've completed the B-CAPs and any additional checklists you feel are appropriate, however your engine is still failed and you are quietly gliding toward the earth. Hopefully you have selected a suitable landing surface and are preparing for a nice and controlled landing at that location. We will discuss landing site selection and some good glide techniques and finding/visualizing the wire in the next chapter. For now however, imagine that you have all that nicely figured out and you're preparing for the touchdown.

At some point you need to secure the engine. What I mean by that is that you need to start shutting off systems and possibly some partial combustion events still happening, and commit to the execution of your pattern and wire and eventual landing.

I'll never tell you to stop restart attempts. If you have the situational awareness to continue to attempt to start the failed engine, and you think it might start…then good on you! Keep doing it. You just never know. Maybe there is something you can do to get the engine going again. Keep on trying, it may not hurt anything, and you could certainly salvage what is about to be a really bad day.

However, if you are like me, at some point it will be time to stop all of that and focus on the mechanics of the glide and your flightpath as well as the landing phase and touchdown. If your restart attempts are causing you to look inside more and your glide path and wire, or airspeed control start to unravel, it will be time to forego the restarts and fly the damn plane! Remember our EP hierarchy mantra from USAF pilot training? Maintain aircraft control is always first! So do that and continue to update and adjust your glide path to arrive safely at your point of intended touchdown.

Once you are committed, it will be time to secure the engine and airplane. Typical steps for most GA aircraft involve setting the mixture to cut-off to prevent more fuel for traveling up to the engine, turning off the electrical system, activating an

ELT if you have controls in the cockpit to do so, and possibly opening the door(s) to prevent airframe bending from effectively sealing or locking the door(s) shut.

For the V35, the POH recommends the following steps for LANDING WITHOUT POWER. The A36 checklist is similar:

1. Airspeed - 83 kts / 96 mph
2. Fuel Selector - OFF
3. Mixture - IDLE CUT-OFF
4. Magneto/start Switch - OFF
5. Flaps - AS REQUIRED
6. Landing Gear - DOWN OR UP, TERRAIN DEPENDENT
7. Battery & Alternator Switches - OFF

This checklist, for me, is adequate. Again, getting the fuel delivery turned off and the magnetos and electrical systems turned off are the highlights of this checklist. As I stated above, I'd add that ELT activation step perhaps and possibly open the door. The A36 checklist does add the ELT step.

Interestingly, the checklist calls for a speed of 83 kts or 96 mph. A note in the checklist calls for this higher than normal speed to "assure the availability of control during the flare." This philosophy makes sense, and we talked about the similar "cash it in" acceleration maneuver in the F-16 when on short final during SFOs for just this very reason. However, I am confused about these Bonanza POH listed speeds as the Engine

Loss checklist procedures have me gliding at 105 KIAS already, and assuming that is going just peachy, I will hold that airspeed (best glide airspeed) all the way to the flare.

Flaps and Gear: Drop 'em?

Let's dig a little deeper into the last three steps of the landing without power checklist. I often hear many different techniques and thoughts on what to do with the gear and flaps when it comes to landing an engine out aircraft. If you have fixed gear, then that part of the decision is already made for you, but you have flaps to consider too. We'll wrap it up with a discussion on the electrical system and why that is the final step in the checklist.

So the gear, what do we do with them? You are approaching your landing point engine out and you need to decide. You only get one shot at this. Lowering the gear will significantly increase your drag, and subsequent glide ratio. But maybe they will help absorb energy in the touchdown/impact. In the Bonanza, we can lower the gear on battery power alone. (Remember this is not recommended during normal operations. The ABS recommends that if you ever lower gear on battery power alone, that you should run the alternate gear extension checklist too, just to be sure they are fully down and locked). Remember, after the engine quits, the alternator quits too, and you will be left with the systems that you typically see during start-up when you flick the battery and alternator (or master) switches to the ON position.

I'll diverge from the gear discussion for just a second to explain this technique. It makes total sense, but quite often I do not see pilots checking or noting what the battery provides power to during start up ground ops. For my Bonanza, when I turn on battery power I get the engine monitor, exterior lights, gear down and alternator-out lights, and fuel gauges, as well as most avionics…that's about it! Please take a few minutes to look at your single engine bird (maybe even sit in the seat) turn on the battery, and memorize what power you get and don't get to various systems. This is what you will see when the engine fails and you begin your glide.

Okay, so back to the landing gear. You need to make this decision now, today, and stick with it for better or worse. When will you keep them up and when will you put them down? If you are really high on energy, you may in-fact need to put them down to get back down to your wire and avoid an overshoot of the runway or your chosen landing spot.

For me, I will plan on lowering my gear when the "landing is assured" (meaning, I know I can make it) and if the surface is something close to what the gear are designed to land on. If it's a grass or hard-packed dirt field, or a road or runway, I'll lower my gear. If I'm planning a touchdown in water, heavy woods or rocky fields, or even tall cornfields, I will leave the gear up. I'm concerned about snagging the nose gear on something and flipping the aircraft over.

In the final chapter I will present you with some more gear up or down statistics and facts if you are still uncertain about what to do. Additionally, here is what David Jack Kenny of the Air Safety Institute has to say about engine out landings and the use of landing gear during that event:

> "First the good news: Either way, your odds are pretty good, as long as the airplane touches down under positive control. A quick check of five years' worth of forced landings in retracts found that in 84 percent, everyone on board survived. Impacts with the airplane out of control are fatal just about that often. The main tradeoff is between inevitable damage to the airplane - not necessarily catastrophic - in a gear-up landing and more serious injuries if the gear snags and it noses over. The surface below has a lot to do with that. In a gear-down water ditching, a nose over is almost certain. The airplane will be totaled anyway, so keep the wheels up. If you're over a turf farm or deserted highway, though, it's almost a normal landing, so put 'em down. On ranch land, lower the gear only if the terrain

is smooth and free of obstacles like fences or boulders" (as cited in Schmelzer, 2012).

So what about using flaps when engine out? I say use them, but be careful, and only when the energy situation dictates you can use them. The FAA's Airplane Flying Handbook recommends the following for flaps and the engine-out approach. "Since flaps improve maneuverability at slow speed, and lower the stalling speed, their use during final approach is recommended when time and circumstances permit" (Airplane Flying Handbook, 2004). Not super helpful, huh?

We need to understand though, that the timing and use of the flaps must be carefully planned for. Additionally, once the flaps are down, you never want to retract them. Chances are you're already slow, and doing so will drastically reduce your lift. If you lower the flaps early, and subsequently realize that you are low and slow, accept the fact that they are down and the resulting slower speed they will permit during your touchdown, even if it means landing short.

Much like the landing gear, the flaps are a commitment. Once they are down they should stay there. Personally, I plan to use flaps on very short final as long as I am not slow. I plan on rolling them to full in one motion and using their added lift and drag to help cushion my touchdown. If you should roll them down early, be prepared to have a very steep approach and possibly find yourself slow. You will also bleed airspeed extremely quickly once in the round out and flare with flaps extended under no power.

The bottom line is that you need to make the decision today, and think about that decision during your training and practice. There are a lot of factors to consider with both the gear and the flaps. I have presented you with my suggestions based on some research, but you will need to decide for yourself, what you think will be best for you. More on the gear up or down debate in the next chapter.

Okay, so when do we do the final step of this checklist and secure the electrical system? The primary reason for doing this step at all, is to hopefully avoid any increased chance of a post-crash (errr...post touchdown) fire. In the Bonanza, with electrical power off, you pretty much have nothing but pneumatic controlled instruments (airspeed, altitude, and VVI) remaining. The landing gear and flaps will be frozen where they are. Lights and radios will also go quiet too.

Mr. Jamie MacDougall whose engine loss story is in the next section, mentioned to me once that when he committed to turning the battery off during his engine loss scenario that things got really quiet. *Really quiet.* He could hear nothing but the sound of wind rushing past the airplane and whistling through small openings and cracks. Be prepared for this step, there really is no turning back at that point.

Because the checklist doesn't say when to do this step, I would recommend a few things to consider for your decision making and planning processes. First, in the Bonanza, you will have no stall warning when the electrical is turned off (and no AoA in most applications). This is important! That air-powered airspeed indicator will be all you have left protecting you from the stall as you complete this procedure and landing. Please look at your systems in your aircraft of choice and figure out if your stall warning device is wired to the battery, or not.

Secondly, I would ensure that my gear and flaps are set where I want them before shutting down master power. I can always flick the battery back on and adjust gear or flaps in the Bonanza, however in a real situation, gliding toward the earth, I am fairly certain that I won't have the brain-power or skill to accomplish that feat. Get the gear and flaps where you want them to be, and then somewhere close to short final, when you're ready, turn off the electrical system. And remember, if you are lowering flaps extremely late in the approach because you didn't want to get low and slow (or maybe you were already low and slow and decided to keep them up), then you could be turning off the electrical system quite literally as you ready to flare.

The Engine Out Flare

The flare during an engine out landing can be quite critical for obvious reasons. Hopefully by this point you have selected your point of intended touchdown and you have made it there. Your goal at this point is to land the plane, nothing more.

The sight picture will be different than what you are used to seeing. Remember, you will be coming down at nearly 1,500 fpm and on a six degree wire, or more. This is roughly double what you see on a normal approach. You will notice a fair bit of ground rush, too. Be prepared to begin the flare early and "round out" the descent smoothly. Touching down with a six degree descent and angle may not be something you can walk away from unless you round it out.

Due to the ground rush and unusual steepness of this type of approach, I recommend that you practice a few of these (with a CFI on the first few) so you can get accustomed to the aggressiveness of this approach. It's nothing too cosmic, but it does bear some discussion and planning for, as it can surprise you the first time.

Remember the old Bob Hoover quotation about flying the thing as far into the crash as possible? What Bob was saying was to shallow the angle out as much as possible and attempt to arrive with minimum downforce and impact. At least that's what I think he was trying to get at. A properly timed flare will permit a soft and slow touchdown, which is the goal. Ideally, you will have the yoke fully aft, entering the stall horn regime just as you touch down. But remember you might not have a horn!

You should also be looking out in front of the aircraft at the landing path. In case you are still fast due to your correct engine out airspeed glide, you will now need to lose energy as you transition to high-speed three-wheeler mode. The gear and flaps will assist with this, but be prepared for a float or balloon. If time allows, attempt to steer away from anything hard and aim for the farthest clear point you can see. Continue to hold the aircraft a few feet off the surface, and prepare for the touchdown and possible intense deceleration.

Lastly, it's possible that if you are landing gear down on un-improved terrain or gear up, that the aircraft will skid or possibly tumble. Keeping her straight and without any yaw is about all you can do to avoid any such post touchdown calamity.

We will cover how to practice these steep flares a little more in the next chapter.

IMC and Engine Out

I'd like to take a little bit of a look into engine out landings while IMC. This is an extremely dangerous situation and one that has claimed the life of many pilots. We need to examine it here as well as develop some tactics to counter this threat. The 2012 Nall Report stated that, "More than 60% of all accidents in IMC were fatal compared to just over 15% of those in VMC during daylight hours and 34% of those in VMC at night."

A different report from the NTSB also stated, "The fatality rate for weather-related GA accidents is approximately three times higher than that for all GA accidents, and fatality rates for weather-related GA accidents have been consistently high over the years, ranging between 58% and 72%" (Price – Groff, 2003).

It goes without saying that an engine out situation in IMC is an extremely difficult situation for any pilot. One must be able to do the first step in the engine out mantra through the entire IMC glide. You must "maintain aircraft control" and be able to continuously do so while conducting a gliding descent in the weather. Don't forget you must still do your CAPs and checklists and also try to make it to a survivable position to land. You will need to do this while also maintaining an adequate instrument crosscheck and keep the aircraft safely airborne on the descent profile.

The question is, how do you know what's below you, and what will be a safe place to touchdown once you emerge from the soup?

Mr. Anker recently faced this situation in his A36 Bonanza. He was lucky to have an airfield nearby and higher IMC minimums that were close to 600 feet (AGL). If it wasn't for that, he may have been another statistic. Even ceilings at 600 feet AGL are pretty low for an engine loss scenario.

So how can we prepare for the IMC glide and procedure? First off, training! Go out and get really good at the basics, get comfortable with the procedures, and practice, practice, practice! Secondly, you can pseudo practice IMC engine out scenarios and I will show you how to do that in the following chapter.

The single most significant factor to surviving the IMC engine out is weather minimums. I would recommend that you sit down right now and take an honest look at your skills and mission and determine what your personal IMC minimums will be should you lose the engine. Remember that landing successfully from an engine out situation, while IMC over low minimums (less than 500 feet), is extremely difficult and your chances of survival diminish rapidly with every foot lower the clouds go.

In the F-16 we had dash 1 guidance for IMC FOs. It states that we need to see the runway by 2,000 feet AGL (base key). If not, our guidance is simple. Eject. That was it. In the F-16 a vertical velocity of about 6,000+ fpm was typical for most SFOs or FOs. So if you do the math, we were expected to break out of a 2,000 foot ceiling, engine out, falling like a rock, see the runway environment and correct for any errors, and land the aircraft, all in the span of about 20 seconds from cloud breakout to touchdown. Twenty seconds is not all that much time. You had better have been pretty accurate in your IMC FO execution to make it land-able. I do not know of a single F-16 pilot that ever landed an F-16 from an IMC FO.

Considering all that, and the fact that you probably don't have an ejection seat, may I recommend that you really think about your IMC weather minimums. I know some Experimental aircraft pilots with bubble canopies who do fly with parachutes and the ability to egress inflight, but I do not know of the viability of exiting the aircraft while that low, with a parachute, in a power-off gliding descent.

Let us look and equate the Bonanza vertical velocity in the glide to the F-16. If we say that we are gliding at an easy math VVI of 1,000 fpm in our Bonanza, then 20 seconds equals about 333 feet. I'm not sure about you, but personally I don't like the idea of breaking out underneath the weather at just 333 feet above the ground and then attempting to finish the engine out landing in 20 seconds. To me that seems quite difficult and not very survivable. And what if you don't break out? You do not have that ejection seat backup! For this reason, I am of the camp that believes that we should bump up personal IMC minimums for single engine aircraft. (Not legally or with regulation, but as a course of training and good pilot decision making.)

It depends on terrain as well. If I'm over the farmlands of Iowa, maybe I will accept lower minimums. If I am flying over hostile mountains out west, I'd prefer to bump up my IMC minimums. Are there runways around that you can use, or are you miles from anything populated? It truly all depends. I will not be setting or suggesting IMC glide minimums for you in this book; that tough decision is for you to decide. I will however reiterate that your currency, mission, and payload (kids and family on board?) should all weigh heavily into your decision to fly single engine over any kind IMC.

Aside from some of the training that we will chat about later, there are a few things that you can do to help yourself prepare for any IMC engine out scenario. One, of course, you already read about, it's called Synthetic Vision (SVT). SVT is an incredible piece of technology that can save your life in this situation. SVT has the ability to display a basic attitude indicator with real-world terrain and features (like runways and roads) on a portable device of your choosing. To the un-initiated, it looks like a computer video game. And if you can find the runway on the computer game, you can probably do the same in real life when IMC. Check it out, it's a game-changer. It is quite easy to look at the device screen and use that as the primary reference for the horizon and world when you are unable to see anything outside due to the weather.

Another technique you can do if you don't have SVT is to always have a GPS set to the nearest field as you cruise along. With this option, you might be able to do the math following an engine failure and get yourself in a position to land just based on that math. But that is a difficult endeavor. In the F-16, our FO glide was mathematically convenient. We could glide approximately one nautical mile for every 1,000 feet of altitude. So if I was 10,000 feet AGL and my distance to the field was 10 nm, I would be feeling pretty good. We actually practice SFOs sometimes from a long straight-in where these kinds of numbers are used. The math is easy thank heavens, because the sink rate is incredible.

In your single engine aircraft, the sink rates are not terribly fantastic, but the math and runway alignment can be much more challenging. More on this and similar techniques in the next chapter.

Here are some final notes from Mr. Anker from the day after his event, regarding personal IMC minimums. The decision is ultimately yours.

"We talk about those personal minimums. I have under a thousand hours, accumulated beginning in year 2000 or thereabouts. When I first got my instrument rating, I observed very conservative minimums until I started to get some actual time, then ratcheted it down to "minimums." I would do that without enough practice to be safe, and it was downright stupid. I remember an IMC departure from Ponca one night at 100 & a half, just to impress a girl. I've calmed down a bit since then. A few years, a few more ratings, and a wife will do that to you. Up until yesterday, I still wouldn't have thought much more about it other than "if I'm at an ILS runway, then I won't take off at less than 200 & 1/2." If that had been the case yesterday, then I'd be in that drainage ditch or just plain dead." *Mr. Matt Anker*

What an Engine Failure "Looks Like"

I am sometimes asked what an engine failure in an airplane looks and sounds like. In fact, based on some recent good feedback on my webpage and other internet posts, interested pilots like you, have asked for this information.

Obviously, an engine failure "looks like" a stopped propeller and might "sound like" a big bang or vibration. But that is not always the case. There have been many accidents where the aircraft engine was running rough, or just not developing ample power. In these instances, the engine failure was not as clear-cut and obvious. What you need to realize is that there is truly a spectrum of engine failure varieties and how they might present themselves to you in the cockpit will vary as well. From the horrific bang and stopped propeller, to the insidious CHT indication change, a multitude of events can be described as engine failure or pending engine failure and you will need to know how to identify them.

Modern GA aircraft engine monitors are the foremost method to analyzing your engine performance and catching any pending engine problems. Without an engine monitor, you are simply in the dark as a pilot. You really do need to have a somewhat modern engine monitor if you want to better predict a pending engine problem or failure as well as to monitor the overall health of the engine throughout its lifespan.

Two relatively common engine anomalies are something I'm sure you've heard of before. They're called detonation and preignition. Detonation occurs when the fuel-air mixture spontaneously ignites due to excessive cylinder temperatures. Preignition occurs when cylinder pressures are high during the compression stroke and the fuel-air charge in the cylinder self-ignites early, prior to the normal spark plug firing point. Instead of igniting when the timed spark plugs fire, this early ignition happens for various reasons and can cause significant damage to the cylinder and engine.

During the start of a detonation event, your EGT will decrease and the CHT will increase in the problem cylinder. Without a way to see individual cylinder EGTs or CHTs, this event may go unnoticed to you. "As pilots, we can usually avoid such damage by being alert for the excessive CHT and depressed EGT that is characteristic of detonation, and reacting promptly by reducing power and going to full-rich mixture. An engine monitor is essential here and programming the CHT alarm to go off at 400° will help get your attention and take the appropriate action" (M. Busch, 2013).

A preignition event can be detected in the cockpit as well. "I've now had the opportunity to see numerous preignition events through my company's SavvyAnalysis service (we now have engine monitor data on 1.2 million GA flights from well over 6,000 airplanes). What I've learned is that preignition has a very distinctive signature (CHT rising above 400F at a rate exceeding one degree per second), and that the pilot typically has approximately one minute to detect the condition and throttle back to avoid destruction of the piston and spark plugs. Few pilots are trained to recognize this condition and react immediately, so preignition usually results in destruction of the cylinder. But it doesn't have to if the pilot understands how to detect a pre-ignition event and to take corrective action immediately" (M. Busch, personal communication, July 2016).

Here are a few other things to consider when we look at ways in which an engine can fail, and what it might look like to you in the cockpit. Mr. John Deakin of Advanced Pilot Seminars (APS) who has years of engine experience and piston engine test involvement permitted me to pass along some of his very knowledgeable thoughts on what is actually happening inside the engine when a detonation event goes bad. He says that sometimes, something in the cylinder can cause "a hot spot to develop on or near the plug. This initiates an abnormal combustion event well before it should occur, as the piston rises on the compression stroke. It may occur at, say, 30 or 40 degrees before Top Dead Center, or more. That causes a massive blow to the top of the piston, which is like the hammer of Thor. Once that starts, successive combustion events become much worse. CHT in that cylinder rises *very* rapidly (1 to 3 degrees Fahrenheit per second) and as the CHT goes through the limits, the piston (Aluminum) begins to disintegrate, at first spitting the bits out the exhaust. Perhaps in 30 seconds to a minute, this will eat a hole in the piston face, and now the real fun begins." (Deakin, 2016).

He continues by stating that at this point in the event, there is nothing abnormal in the cockpit except for the rising CHT. There will be no oil pressure anomalies, or even pilot-detectable engine roughness. Soon, the piston face disintegrates, compressions are lost and oil and vapor now begins to pour out of the breather and overboard "and the engine starts shaking, a little. Deep inside the engine, bearings get hot. Really hot, very quickly. Red hot. Then white hot!" (Deakin, 2016). As the oil is lost and parts overheat, the engine will begin to destroy itself, and it's only a matter of time before a rod bearing, or crankshaft bearing, or some other component completely fails.

This is why an engine monitor is critical, as mentioned above. One of the only ways you can tell that your engine is failing, initially, might be that CHT spike or alarm.

While it would be nice to outline all the ways in which an engine could fail, and all the possible indications in the cockpit, that task is just too great. There are too many variables. I do believe that a pending engine failure will manifest in some way on a modern engine monitor most of the time, and any anomalous indications should warrant investigation and possibly an immediate turn toward your nearest Key position (more on that next) while gaining as much altitude as you possibly can. Keeping a watchful eye on all of your cylinders and EGTs, and looking for out-of-place changes or differences is a great way to detect an engine problem or potential failure early. But also remember that sometimes the engine can fail instantly, with no advance warning on an engine monitor or otherwise. You will read about a real-world case in the next section where that happened exactly.

The bottom line is that there are a full spectrum of engine failure types, and you need all the tools and tactics at your disposal to handle the situation with talent.

Final Thoughts

In this chapter we have talked about some pretty ordinary checklists and examined some engine out checklists and procedures for the mighty F-16. We have looked at some of the reasoning behind the checklists for the Bonanza and developed a hopefully useful set of B-CAPs for the Bonanza and most GA single engine airplanes. We also looked at some energy management techniques and optimistically you should now have a much better understanding of energy management and some of the concepts therein as they apply to the engine out glide.

If you are not entirely familiar with the checklists in your aircraft, now would be the time to examine them and compare our recommended B-CAPs to what your POH says. We have also looked at a few ways in which an engine failure can manifest, and what those indications might look like in the cockpit.

With all this good information at the forefront of your mind, now is the time to begin our inflight training. It's always good to have the "book knowledge," but now it is imperative that you take what we have covered and apply it to the real world in the seat of your airplane, and practice these techniques so you are armed for the day it really happens.

In this next chapter, I will show you how.

ENGINE OUT TRAINING AND PRACTICE

I now understand the wisdom of not taking passengers up on the first flight after major maintenance.

I just got the plane back from getting the starter adapter overhauled, and I took her up for the shakedown cruise. I was climbing through 5,500 feet when all of a sudden the engine started running extremely rough. I had about two seconds of denial run through my mind, then all the training kicked in.

I switched tanks, tried the mags, moved the throttle, turned fuel pump on and off, all to no avail. That's when I smelled a very strong smell of fuel in the cockpit. I was monitoring approach, and then said the words I never thought I'd actually have to say, "Mayday Mayday Mayday!"

I was out over the San Fernando Valley and could see Van Nuys airport, so I told them that's where I was going. By this point I had pulled power to idle which reduced the shaking, set up best glide, and then did the second thing I thought I'd never have to do which was secure the engine, pull the mixture to idle cutoff and turn off the fuel selector. The controller seemed more stunned than I was, as it seemed it took her a while to respond. She asked if I had the tower frequency. I was too busy to look it up, so I asked her to give it to me. I switched to tower while I was setting up to approach to glide in and used the "mayday" word again and told them I could smell fuel.

They cleared me to land on any runway. When I knew I had the runway made, I put the gear down and shut all the electrical off and unlatched the door. I can't tell you how eerily quiet it got at that point, except for the sound of my heartbeat. I made a greaser landing and even had enough energy remaining to coast off the runway onto the ramp.

I believe I ran the 100 yard dash out of the plane in about 0.2 seconds. Meanwhile there were about half a dozen fire trucks and another half dozen airport police rolling, but thankfully fire department intervention was unnecessary.

It took about two minutes of standing on terra firma for the hand shaking and knee-knocking to begin. Up until that point I think I had been as calm as a cucumber.

At this point, I [couldn't] see anything obvious in the engine compartment that might have caused this emergency to occur.

Other Notes: I just did what I had been taught to do. Honestly, everything was happening so fast and I had to make so many decisions so quickly. I didn't have time to actually think about it... not until later anyway.

I wasn't looking at engine instruments when it suddenly started running rough, since at that point the engine was running like a top, so I had my eyeballs looking outside during the climb, where eyeballs should be. But, as I started trying to trouble-shoot, I glanced down at the engine monitor. The JPI-700 display which normally shows lots of orange bars of happiness was not right at all. Instead, it was basically all blackness, except for an occasional 1-bar flicker on an occasional cylinder, and if I recall correctly, the EGTs were only showing a few hundred degrees instead of the normal 1400s-1500s, so I realized very little combustion was occurring.

Then the fuel smell came.

I knew from the visual picture of having practiced engine out glides that I had enough altitude to make the airport; but honestly, securing the engine and turning off the fuel selector provided a sort of gut-wrenching "this is REALLY the real deal" finality to that particular decision. I had also practiced power-off descents to the runway from above the pattern many times, but during those exercises it is (in hindsight) very different because I know if I screw up I can just add power and try again. Also, unlike during the practicing of power-off to the runway when you are sort of mentally checking off altitudes as you descend to make sure you are hitting your energy targets, I really just did this by eyeballing it and thinking, "at this point in relation to where the runway is, this looks about right."

Post thoughts: I am very thankful to have walked away from this unscathed, but I didn't survive because of luck. (Okay, well maybe I was a little bit lucky.) Mostly, it was the frequent training for emergencies over the years that allowed me to act reflexively.

I hope none of you ever have to experience something like this, but if you do, the best advice I can give you is **STAY CALM, think, and rely on your training.** Staying calm is what really saved my life, and as a result, the outcome was a non-event...except for a good story!

With permission by Mr. Jamie MacDougall, 1979
Bonanza A36TN

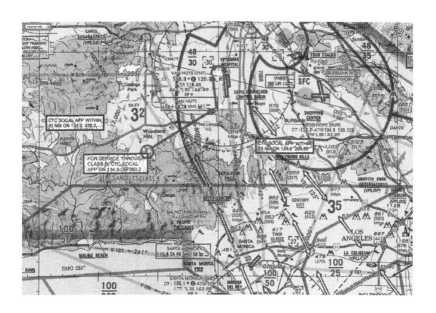

There's simply no substitute for experience in terms of aviation safety. – Chesley Sullenberger

Training and Practice Basics

In this chapter we are going to examine almost every aspect of training and practice for engine out situations. As you read above, Mr. MacDougall believes that his frequent training for glides and engine out procedures is what really saved his bacon that fateful day. I would argue that any pilot who has successfully recovered from an engine loss inflight would probably say the same.

I would like to expose you to multiple different training techniques and examples. We will look at them all and you are free to decide what you like, what doesn't work for you, and what works for you in your single engine aircraft of choice. Hopefully, you can develop a solid training regimen and use multiple techniques from below to expand your personal knowledge and stick and rudder skills, and ultimately your *experience*, to have those skills ready and sharp in case you ever need to use them.

Basic Numbers and Settings

Let us first take a look as some baseline glide numbers and some pitch and power settings that you can use when you are ready to practice your flameouts and simulated flameouts (SFOs). Before we do however, I believe that we need to first know how far we can glide. That's easy right? For the Bonanza we've already stated that the clean glide ratio is 1.7 nm per 1,000 feet of altitude. Hopefully you already know your numbers for your single engine aircraft. (You'd better, I told you to get those figured out in Chapter One!)

But seriously, those numbers are great, and you need to know them. However, I'd like you to put yourself into the following scenario.

Imagine that you are flying over some rocky terrain out west. You're not sure what the elevation of those cacti and rocks are below, but you can guess that it's between 3,000 and 4,000 feet MSL, and your charts seem to help you determine that as well. But you're not sure *exactly*. You are at 8,500 MSL and you've got some open fields and a road out the left window and you know there is an airfield off the nose, but you can't quite make it out yet. Over to the right side of the aircraft you can't see much in the way of possible landing locations, and the wing is blocking most of your field of view anyway.

If your engine was to quit *right then*, could you make any of those viable landing spots? Could you? How do you know?

Without knowing the exact elevation of the landing spot, and your exact distance to that spot, you really can't do the math to determine if you could glide there or not. You might as well throw those snazzy book numbers out the window, huh?

You will see that during your training, and in some of the examples below, that we will in fact use known and measured references on the ground. I'd recommend figuring out exact elevations and even building some "User" points into your GPS database for those points. When it comes to practice, especially initial practice, knowing the numbers and flying to them is a great way to start. It's a good reinforcement and a good way to learn. There are also some programs on the internet that can help you find elevations and GPS coordinates for various spots on the earth. Or, if you have your favorite uncontrolled and quiet airfield, you can go out to the edge of the runway with a handheld GPS, or use the one in your aircraft to capture some solid and known GPS points.

I highly recommend that you also build a few local known points that you can reference and practice gliding to when you need to. Even flying past one or two known and measured spots on your way to your favorite fly-in breakfast spot can help you develop the sight picture for how far you could glide.

In the real world though, I doubt that you will have known GPS points and altitudes to random fields everywhere you fly. What about the "nearest" functions that some GPS devices tout? Will those not help? I am a huge fan of dialing in the nearest airfield into the GPS. This allows both a general awareness of that airfield and its position relative to me as well as having some distance numbers to that field that I can calculate glide math to, to determine if I can make it or not. But often, I do not have all possible airfields loaded into my GPS as it's sometimes just not high on the cockpit priority task list. Additionally, there are no GPS points to that grassy field off at your seven o'clock that you are just now passing by.

So again, how do you *truly* know, you can make that patch of grass or distant runway, and do so safely?

I talked about the engine loss situation more with Mr. MacDougall and he informed me that during his event he just didn't have enough time or "brain bytes" to load Van Nuys airfield into his GPS system. I do not blame him. Personally, I do not think that I could load anything into a GPS after recognition and handling of an engine failure. There would be just too much to do and pilot task load would be too great. His panel was also shaking like a pissed off cat, and he stated that initially reading any of the gauges or GPS numbers was nearly impossible.

So how do we know we can make it to that field, Buster? How can a pilot be certain that a landing spot is reachable, in a hurry, under duress with a coughing or sputtering (or failed) engine?

Mr. MacDougall said, "It just looked about right." Yes, with lots of training and practice, it will look just about right for you as well.

Remember our earlier discussion on getting comfortable with a three degree wire on a normal approach? I bet that you could go out right now and fly a normal visual approach to any runway, and you would be able to tell me if we were high and steep or low and shallow. Would you agree?

What I'm getting at is something fighter pilots call "sight picture." You need to develop an accurate sight picture for what the glide looks like, and then refine that sight picture with repeated practice so it becomes burned into your brain.

How do we begin to develop this sight picture? One way we can figure this all out is by determining the glide angle (or wire) we will need to fly for our airplane in a glide. Some basic math tells us that for the Bonanza, 1.7/1,000 feet or a 10 to 1 glide ratio will equate to a 5.5 degree angle of descent. See figure 13.

Best Glide Angle
Figure 13

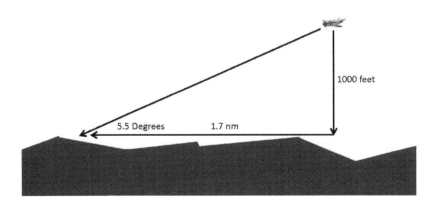

1000 feet

5.5 Degrees   1.7 nm

So for our nominal glide we will be on a 5.5 wire, if everything is working as advertised and you are not gear down or something. For the sake of argument, let's say that we will use a six degree wire. It's worth talking about here that the 5.5 degree wire may in fact be what the Bonanza will accomplish, under perfect conditions. However, realize that during an actual emergency we as humans will be late to actually recognize the event and commit to it. Some studies actually say that true detection time and pilot reaction time to a critical emergency in an aircraft can take from three to five seconds, or more. One may also forget to close the cowl flaps, or maybe the engine is windmilling and you can't get the prop back to coarse, or you forget to do so until later in the situation. Any way you look at it, mistakes will be made in the execution of a perfect textbook glide, and your subsequent glide angle will steepen.

Hopefully our training helps us eliminate most or all of those mistakes, however we are all imperfect. For those reasons, I use a six degree glidepath for my planning, training and estimations. I ask you to determine your glide angle for your chosen and trusty steed now. (Hint: Most Cessnas and GA birds are six degrees too.)

I rely on two unique methods for determining what six degrees looks like in my airplane. Our friends in the astronomy field have developed some pretty reliable and accurate methods for easily determining degrees and degrees apart for objects in the sky. Fortunately, we can use their celestial wizardry in our humble airplanes.

This first method I call the "Hand Method." As long as you don't have the hands of a giant and the arms of a monkey, you should be able to use these interesting techniques, too. According to the astronomy gurus, if you hold your arm out straight and turn your wrist 90 degrees as to look at the top of your hand, various fingers and widths of fingers can actually determine degrees. See figure 14 for examples.

Hand Method
Figure 14

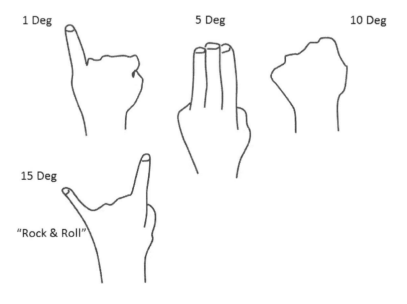

So somewhere between three fingers and a closed fist, we can find six degrees. For me about four fingers equals six degrees. You can use the below Big Dipper chart in figure 15 to "calibrate" your hand, and see how this technique works for your arm and hand. I was surprised how accurate it really is.

Big Dipper
Figure 15

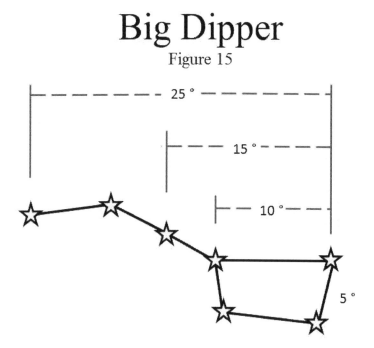

While airborne, stable, and level, hold your arm outstretched, with four fingers together. Hold it just below the horizon and note the first piece of land you can see below your four fingers, and THAT should be the no-wind range you can glide! Realistically, if you use three fingers or four, or something in the middle, it will be close for your Bonanza or single engine aircraft.

I went out and did some test glides in my aircraft during the course of writing this book (more on that later), and I found that on a measured course with measured distances, altitudes and glides that my four finger technique was really close to where I actually glided to, every time.

Winds, bumps, and our inaccurate eyeballs also play a factor into this technique, and this entire hand exercise is simply an estimate. But it will give you a really good and quick idea of how far you can make it and ultimately help you determine the correct engine-out sight picture that you will soon develop. Give it a try!

My other tried and true method for determining glide range quickly and accurately is something I call the "Wingtip Method." If you use the hand method to determine a spot you can glide to, overlay your right hand with four fingers over your right wing (low wing airplane). Note a point on the wing where six degrees below the horizon sits. That point on the wing now will not change as long as your sitting height doesn't change and you are in level flight. You can even do this technique while on the ground or in the chocks, and identify spots on both wings that equate to six degrees low.

During my inflight testing, I was able to mathematically put the aircraft on a perfect six degree wire, at an exact altitude and range from a visible target during the setup and start of my tests. Where that visible target fell on a point on my wing was nearly identical to what I found during the hand method technique for a six degree wire. See figure 16 below.

6 Wire

Figure 16

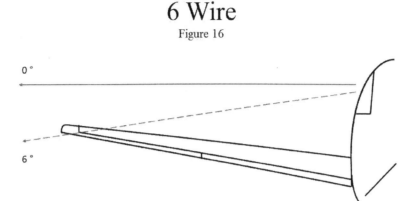

In figure 17, we have a graphical representation for me and my sitting height of what I found to align as six degrees below the horizon on the wingtip. Maybe, I'll even paint a new reference stripe at that point on the wing when I get the airplane repainted someday!

With the Wingtip Method, remember that it only works in level flight, but it works over any terrain and at any altitude. Additionally, once you can visualize the points on each wing that correspond to your glide angle, you can do one more interesting thing. This one is a little trickier and not as accurate, but it also works. Draw an imaginary circle around your airplane at that six degree depression by connecting the points on each wingtip. With your new imaginary circle, you can see now that anything inside that circle will be something you can glide to! Think about that glide ring or imaginary circle as you go flying next time, and practice that visualization each time you fly. Before you know it, that far off grassy field "will look about right."

There is a third method for our Cessna, Cub, and Husky drivers. Sorry if I forgot anyone, but basically anyone with a high wing airplane that has no dihedral can use the following technique to determine gliding range. I call this method the "Wing Dip" method.

Using a standard Cessna 172 for example, the POH says that it will glide 1.5 nm for every 1,000 feet of vertical (propeller windmilling, no flaps, no wind). Applying some math shows us that the above glide ratio delivers a 6.2 degree glidepath or wire for the average Cessna 172. You can see, about six degrees works again for training and practice for you Cessna guys and gals.

For you high wing folks, when flying along straight and level, simply roll into six degrees of bank on your ADI (or the bank angle you determine to be your average glide wire). Look out the window at a point about six or so inches below the wingtip lower edge and magically you have found your approximate glide distance on the earth. You are simply using the wings as an aiming reference for six degrees below the horizon. This also works at any altitude, over any terrain. See figure 18 for an example.

Wing Dip Method
Figure 18

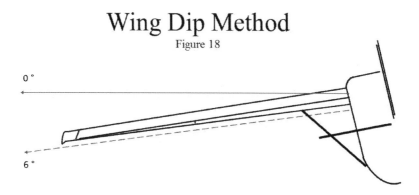

The Wing Dip method is a little more cumbersome, and it only works for high wing aircraft as most low wing birds seem to have some amount of wing dihedral. And for the high wing driver, you actually have to do the six degree bank accurately to visualize max gliding range which could prove cumbersome during an actual engine out, heavy vibration, and heavy task load situation. But with some practice, you might be able to also do some rehearsal visualizations and generate your own glide ring around your aircraft, and get a feel for that sight picture and a sense of where you can glide to should you ever need to know. You might also be able to find a six degree wire reference off your wing strut or jury struts when in level flight.

Go out and give it a try, and see what you think. I'd be interested to hear what you high wing pilots think and any feedback on how useful or useless this method is.

Real-World Flight Test

While working on this book I decided to go out and fly my Bonanza and get some real-world test data on glides and performance. I know that the Bonanza's glide and performance is heavily documented and described in multiple sources, but I wanted more.

Honestly, I wanted to know what the real world glide numbers were in my plane and then see how they compared to the "book" numbers, and the glide numbers in various other publications. Specifically, I also wanted to know what sort of glide I could get at just idle clean and idle dirty (meaning gear down), and were those settings even close to anything real world that I could use for training? My concern was, for instance, why bother training at idle power and clean if that glide performance happens to be grossly different from any of the real engine out glides we have data for? Is *that* pitch and power setting even relevant to engine out training? Mr. MacDougall stated to me that his actual glide performance on that day "looked" a bit different from what he trained to. As advanced glide concept trainees reading this book, we need to know how to eliminate any differences from a real-world engine loss and our artificial training attempts. We need to practice with the same performance and sight pictures that we predict we would see if faced with a real engine loss situation. There is limited use in training for an engine loss if we can't even simulate it accurately.

I picked a cool and calm morning and fueled up the Bonanza. I also carefully calculated my gross weight for the takeoff and subsequent fuel load that I would have once established and ready in the practice area. I bugged my new best glide airspeed and all of my glides were flown at this new "weight adjusted" airspeed, exactly as described in our first chapter.

The test plan utilized a known point on the ground which I have used for years for engine out training. My known point is exactly 3,000 feet MSL and at the start of a road straightaway following a large curve. This road straightaway is my simulated runway. I also have exact GPS coordinates for this road point and those are loaded into my GPS which also displays ground range (not slant range) distance from the aircraft to that point on multiple avionics down to the 1/10th of a mile. The figure 19 graphic shows my test setup parameters, but basically I calculated and used a starting point 4,000 feet above the target point and 6.8 nm away. (4 x 1.7). Starting at this point and entering the glide, I should theoretically be able to easily glide to my target point or simulated "brick one" of the runway by covering 1.7 nm per every 1,000 feet of altitude.

Starting airspeed was 100-110 KIAS on a 7.0 nm arc from the target point. I'd confirm a clean aircraft and then turn toward the target point while reducing power and establishing the parameters I was testing for on that test run. I would also slow to target airspeed in the turn to be at best glide airspeed at 6.8 nm when pointed at the target to begin my test run.

Flight Test
Figure 19

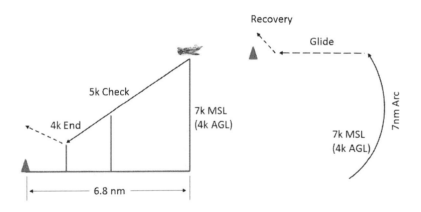

I flew four different glide profiles as to reproduce all engine out aspects and sight pictures that one might see during training or a real-world engine loss event.

1. Idle Clean Prop Windmilling
2. ABS Recommended

3. Idle Gear Down Prop Windmilling

4. Idle Clean Prop Back (Coarse)

The American Bonanza Society (ABS) recommends the following engine settings for Bonanzas during engine out training. These parameters replicate a clean glide with the propeller lever fully aft (not windmilling) but preserve engine speed and temperatures vice setting idle power and rapidly cooling down the engine. ABS also recommends for us Continental engine operators to not perform long, extended power off glides where the airplane is pushing the propeller instead of the propeller pulling the airplane. Their practice glide settings recommended for the Bonanza are: 15" manifold pressure, 2,500 RPM, gear down, and flaps 10 degrees. Then fine tune the MP for about 800-900 feet per minute vertical descent rate. We'll take a closer look at this and the other profiles, how they compared, and what results they produced below.

The outcomes of my tests are interesting. (Well, I think they are at least!) On each run I began at 6.8 nm from the target point and 7,000 feet MSL (4,000 feet AGL) above that target. This is an exact 1.7 nm per 1,000 feet position. Once stabilized downhill on the glide, I checked and recorded my DME to the simulated runway point at 5,000 feet MSL (2,000 feet AGL) and then again at 4,000 feet MSL (1,000 feet AGL), after which I terminated the test run and begun a climb back for the next run. Using the 5,000 MSL "check point" and the 4,000

MSL "final" point allowed for two data points to be gathered on each run. In this way an average glide calculation from start to finish as well as start to the "check point" could be collected and compared.

My first run was Idle Clean (prop 2,500 RPM at start). This test was designed to simulate a clean glide with a windmilling propeller. Passing 5k MSL, I recorded 3.6 DME to go and at the termination point at 4k MSL I saw 2.4 DME to go. Doing the math for both points resulted in 1.6 and 1.46 nautical miles covered for every 1,000 feet of altitude. Pretty close to the predicted outcome! I flew almost the book answer of 1.7 per 1,000 feet, but just a touch worse. Additionally, the resulting vertical velocity (VV) for this glide simulation was 1,200 fpm.

My second run (flown twice actually) was done flying the ABS recommended parameters. This second run resulted in a very shallow descent gradient, as I purposely set 15" MP, but did not adjust it later for the recommended VV. I saw about 600 fpm VV and my final numbers were much better than "book glide." I was getting well over 2 nautical miles per 1,000 feet. Apparently 15" of MP is too high for my aircraft for this simulated glide, and the ABS recommended VV makes that glide far more accurate and realistic.

I decided to run that test glide again and this time reduced power back to 11-12" MP which gave me an ABS recommended 800-900 fpm VV. Once I did that I saw and measured resultant glide ratios of 1.9 nm and 1.8 nm respectively, which are nearly identical to the book.

My third run was Idle and Gear Down (prop 2,500 RMP at start). This test was designed to simulate a "worst case" glide with gear down and prop windmilling. This will also likely simulate what kind of glide you can expect once you drop the gear (terrain dependent) and make your commitment to landing. In this test, as you can guess, I saw some pretty healthy descent numbers. I recorded 1,500 fpm VV and my final glide ratio math came out to 1.15 nm and 1.2 nm per 1,000 feet of altitude lost. This is, of course, far worse than the book.

My fourth and final run was an Idle Clean and Prop all the way back (coarse) test. I wanted to see how my plane performed and compared to the book and how much difference having the prop pulled back can affect glide ratio. On this test I saw 800 fpm VV and the end result resulted in a shave over 2 nm (2.05 nm to be exact) per 1,000 feet of altitude lost overall.

The results of all these tests are summarized in the table below (figure 20). Of note, the column on the far right titled Calculated Wire is simply the resulting math calculation from the numbers I found inflight. This column demonstrates the variability of all four glide profile wires, and what you could be faced with on any given day given an engine loss.

Glide Results
Figure 20

Configuration	Vertical Velocity	Distance / 1000'	Calculated Wire
Idle Clean (prop flat)	1,200 fpm	1.5 nm	6.26
ABS (11-12" MP)	900 fpm	1.8 nm	5.22
Idle Gear Dn (prop flat)	1,500 fpm	1.2 nm	7.81
Idle Clean (prop coarse)	800 fpm	2 nm	4.70

There are a few key points that I would like highlight from this test, some takeaways, and some applications we can use for our future glide training.

The first point is that the ABS numbers work. However, you will need to figure out what settings are similar in your aircraft. When I saw 800-900 fpm VV my results were extremely close to the book numbers for a Bonanza glide. I speculate that for me, about 1,000 fpm VV will pretty much nail the published 1.7 nm per 1,000 feet POH book numbers.

The second important takeaway is that with the propeller pulled back, you can improve (lessen) your descent rate by about 100 fpm. For me this equated to about a 15% gain in glide distance over the book numbers with the propeller knob aft. That was excellent to witness.

The third key takeaway was that in the worst case scenario (Idle, Dirty and Windmilling prop), I saw *roughly* a 1 nm per 1,000 feet descent profile. Sounds like the F-16 ratio right? That, to me sounds like an easy relationship to memorize should I ever find myself very high on energy.

And the final important piece of information that I discovered in doing this test, might be my most poignant. When faced with a real-world engine loss situation, you just don't know what you are going to get for a glide. I think we can make some educated guesses, but in reality you will not know with certainty what to expect. What are the winds going to do to you? Are your gear up or down? What about the propeller, is it windmilling or can you get the lever back and get that thing feathered? There are a lot of uncertainties.

Having multiple different sight pictures and descent gradients "ready and armed" in your repertoire will greatly assist you for the day you lose your engine. You'll have plenty of glide angle tools in your bag of tricks to pull from. That being said however, we will soon identify two "best guess" profiles that you can use for realistic glide exercises and commit them to memory.

Pitch and Power

So what are some real-world "pitch and power" settings and profiles that you can use as you begin your glide training regimen? What I mean by pitch and power is simply power and configuration settings that you can set in your aircraft that are pertinent and realistic to some real-world known glide parameters. Some folks refer to these known settings as "parking the aircraft" or putting it into a known setting and configuration to attain expected airspeed and attitude results. How do we park the aircraft for a practice glide?

I would highly recommend using the ABS numbers for your glide training, or similar parameters that you test and conclude work well for you. These settings do a fantastic job of keeping the engine happy and retaining some heat in the cylinders. In fact, during my glide tests at idle power, my cylinder CHTs dropped to the bottom of the screen, and I was getting some "CHT cold" warnings (below 200 deg F) on my engine monitor. While I'm not a believer in the shock cooling theories, I still wasn't too happy to see the temperatures fall off that much. Personally, I like to keep my temps a little warmer and make slow changes to my engine to allow for better transitions between gross temperature differences.

The ABS settings will be (and always have been) my go-to practice glide configuration. That is where I park the aircraft for my glide practice. We will call this the ABS glide or Glide Profile #1. For my particular aircraft, 15" MP was too much. I would recommend the ABS numbers with the caveat of adjusting the MP to get approximately 900 - 1,000 fpm VV. That setting seems to be a good tradeoff between engine temperature control and correctly replicating the nominal glide. Additionally, I will always hope that I could get the propeller pulled back to coarse during an actual engine loss, but I would not count on it. With that in mind, a 1,000-1,200 fpm VV is an excellent place to simulate a real engine loss (clean configuration) with a windmilling propeller. Remember my Idle Clean glide profile, in Profile #1? It showed us a glide ratio of nearly the book numbers, just slightly worse and 1,200 fpm VV. You could easily simulate that profile with the ABS settings and just reduce MP a little bit more for your desired VV if you chose. But for our training, I'd recommend the ABS glide numbers and a VV of 900 - 1,000 fpm.

My second location to "park the aircraft" is at that worst case situation VV that we covered. If during a real engine out scenario, prop pulled back or not, at some point I am probably going to have to lower the gear (terrain dependent). If that is the case, I will probably be somewhere close to that one-to-one wire we discussed earlier in order to land the plane. Remember that this ratio is not a true one-to-one glide ratio, but a simplistic mathematical one-to-one numerical relationship. 1 nm per 1,000 feet of altitude.

If this is the case, and you want to train to that steeper worst case pitch and power setting, the only change from the ABS nominal glide (Profile #1) to the worst case glide (Profile #2)… is power. Pretty easy right? Just pull the power to idle and the aircraft will perform just as in my worst case glide profile and darn near, if not identical, to the real-world worst case glide. The drag is already out, and the propeller is already windmilling. Think of this second location as "the ABS Glide, Minus Power." It should be an easy transition and easy on pilot workload when nearing Low Key or Base Key. Of note, as seen in the chart above, the worst case glide #2 will mathematically produce about an eight degree wire.

When we start to practice these glides and you decide that you would drop the gear in real life, just set idle power. Below, figure 21 shows a depiction of these two practice glide settings and how they might relate to a landing surface.

Baseline Glides
Figure 21

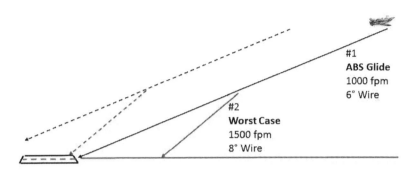

In summary, I recommend two distinctly different glide execution parameters and configurations. Each represents a realistic glide at two different wires based on realistic and probable engine out glide scenarios that you could face.

If you are not a Bonanza operator, all is not lost. You can easily go out one day in your single engine airplane and attempt to find some numbers and power settings that specifically work for you. If you have fixed gear, it's pretty simple, you can probably just pull the power to idle and trim for your weight adjusted best glide speed. You may not have the ability to use an increased power setting (for engine temps) as your fixed gear bird might be already pretty slick and not have any more drag devices available. But if you have a variable pitch propeller, you could see what different glide parameters you can get in your fixed gear single with the propeller forward or back.

If you fly a Mooney or a retractable Cessna, basically any aircraft with retractable gear, you should be able to figure out what settings allow for the gear to be down and increased power to replicate the glide parameters for your specific aircraft.

You should also note your aircraft pitch attitude when doing this flight training. While not as precise as AoA, and subject to changes in aircraft weight, this pitch attitude "reference" will be an excellent pseudo-AoA for you to recall and train to. Given a real engine-out situation you can pitch to this approximate pitch "sight picture" and automatically be very close to your best glide airspeed.

Lastly, I would like to take a minute to look at Mr. Anker's IMC engine failure incident a little more and see how it relates to our pitch and power debate. Specifically, what was the performance of his stricken airplane and how does it relate to our training?

In discussing the situation with Mr. Anker, we were able to analyze the FlightAware radar ground tracks and pertinent engine data and come up with some interesting numbers. What we found was that from the time he lost the engine to the time of touchdown was actually about five minutes. He was also at 6,000 feet MSL at the time of the failure and field elevation was 620 feet MSL. So he was 5,380 feet AGL at the time of the engine failure. Knowing this we can mathematically get an average VV for his trip downhill…any guesses on what it was? That's right, 1,055 feet per minute (average). Interesting, huh?

We can also look at his ground track. This took a little bit more fuzzier math but I arrived at a total distance covered of between 7.5 and 8 nm traveled. Knowing that and his total altitude lost, we can also calculate that he glided an average of 1.5 nautical miles per 1,000 feet, and the average glide angle was 6.3 degrees. Pretty amazing stuff, if you ask me.

Bottom line: trust your known glide ratios and book numbers. They work.

Gliding Turn Tests

How much altitude is required, and how much time does it take to turn your airplane in a glide? Is one bank angle far more efficient than another when it comes to gliding turns? During the writing of this book, I went out on another test sortie and attempted to determine the answers to these questions.

Basically, my plan was to set-up a baseline glide in the standard ABS configuration with a 900-1,000 fpm descent, the best glide profile. From there I flew cardinal headings and began turns of varying degrees of bank while recording altitude lost and my copilot recording the time of each turn with a stopwatch. The results are as follows in figure 22.

Glide 180° Turn Test Results
Figure 22

Bank Angle	Time (seconds)	Alt Lost (feet)
30 Degree	34	600
	36	500
	35	500
45 Degree	19	400
	19	300
	20	450
	20	400
60 Degree	14	500
	14	500
	15	500

Looking at the results, it's quite obvious to me that all 180 degree gliding turns lose roughly the same amount of altitude. Given the accuracy of my ham-fisted turns and execution as well as some standard deviation, realistically, 500 feet of altitude loss is a good honest figure during a best case nominal engine out clean glide, for the Bonanza, in a 180 degree turn. It also would seem that the shallow banked turns required more time to do a 180, while the steeper banked turns took less time, that part is simple, right? What wasn't so obvious until analyzing the data later is that in various bank profiles, no one bank angle is particularly better or worse for altitude lost and efficiency.

To clarify, I am *not* talking about the infamous "impossible turn." That is a different subject and deals with engine loss just after takeoff. While that is a hugely important topic to train for, think about, and practice, that subject will not be covered in-depth here. There have been a multitude of studies and real-world flight tests on the impossible turn, and baseline minimum altitudes and currencies to attempt to do that risky maneuver have been established and greatly debated. My turning tests here are simply to outline some baseline altitude loss parameters for different bank angles in a glide. These altitude loss numbers are important for you to know in your aircraft so you do not waste altitude turning at too steep or too shallow of a bank given a real engine loss event.

Let's look at some notes on the impossible turn and how it relates to our turn tactics. The impossible turn, or turn-back to the runway after takeoff and engine loss was heavily tested by two individuals, Professor of Aerospace Engineering Mr. David F. Rogers, and Navy Midshipman (later an Astronaut) Mr. Brent W. Jett. During their testing, they concluded that "a thirty degree coordinated banked turn at an airspeed just above stall velocity results in the best combination of performance and safety. However, the thirty degree banked turn leaves the aircraft at a greater lateral distance from the runway" (Rogers, 1991). The author also later concludes that "a 45 degree bank angle results in a significantly smaller radius of turn which decreases the distance from the runway. The simulator studies indicate that there is a negligible difference in altitude lost during the turn (2 ft. on average out of 340 feet) and only a minor difference in rate-of-sink (73 fpm on average) at completion of the turn between a 30 degree and 45 degree bank angle" (Rogers, 1991).

My point is that I am not attempting to describe the best way to do the impossible turn and make it back to the runway with minimal offset and time when the engine fails shortly after takeoff; that was the subject of Mr. Rogers' study. He was attempting to balance altitude lost with speed of the turn, or turn rate, and distance back to the landing surface. I am not concerned with that for our purposes, but rather with minimum altitude lost in a turn and balancing that with aircraft controllability. While speed of a turn or turn rate is important, it is of lower significance to the pilot of an engine loss event with a little more time and distance available. I am attempting to describe the best method to glide and turn at the same time, with minimal altitude lost. I think you will see that a 30 degree Angle of Bank (AOB) works very well and also allows you to easily prioritize other important cockpit tasks while safely executing a glide. If turning *time* becomes a factor, then 45 degrees might be your best option.

This was a pretty easy test to do, and I'd recommend that you give it a try in your aircraft of choice for generation of some reference numbers you can use.

Bank Angles

There is not much written in the lore about proper bank angles during these engine out maneuvers. Except for the quoted work above, which was about all I could find. Based on what I found during my second set of Bonanza flight tests, I'd honestly say you could "do what you want" with regard to banking during an engine out situation. However that may not be so smart, and here's why.

Altitude lost in all the various turns was about the same regardless of bank angle, this is true. However, I will be the first to admit that anything at or beyond 45 degrees of bank takes an excessive amount of focus and precision. It became really difficult to keep a consistent airspeed and bank angle at 45 degrees and beyond during inflight execution. For this reason, I recommend a 30 degree AOB during your engine out practice, to keep things more controllable and less wild. This 30 degrees AOB plan translates well to our IMC engine out training too, and allows the pilot more time to focus on energy management, airspeed crosscheck, and flightpath adjustments that are critical to the successful recovery of the aircraft.

Additionally, remember that the steeper bank you fly, the more lift is required to maintain a coordinated turn, and the closer you come to that critical angle of attack and possibly a stall-spin type error. So again, for a couple reasons and this one especially, I recommend keeping it simple and using 30 degrees AOB for your engine out practice and real-world execution. 30 degrees AOB also allows for a little more slop in your airspeed control, should you need it.

Typical GA Engine Out Pattern

A rundown of the typical FAA publications for new pilots and CFIs shows that there isn't a whole lot of information for the average GA pilot on engine out training. The FAA Instructor Handbook and the Student Pilot Guide both do not even mention engine out emergency training. The FAA's Airplane Flying Handbook does illustrate some basic 90, 180 and 360 Power-Off approaches, but these references are quite generic and meant to apply to all kinds of GA aircraft. Additionally, a power-off 180 is required in the commercial pilot practical test standards, but that is it.

While the theory and thought in the FAA Airplane Flying Handbook are sound, they are too simplified. The Handbook does not teach us how to set up a glide or use checklist procedures, and there is no mention of energy management techniques and glide sight pictures. I do not like some of the altitude and numbers given in the Handbook, again it is really a much generalized document.

Additionally, the pattern depictions in the Handbook are portrayed as perfect rectangular "box" patterns, while the literature mentions a circular glidepath at one point. Which is it? There are also too few discussions on altitudes and zero discussion about adjusting the ground track or use of any kind of energy management techniques.

I am not saying that the FAA Airplane Flying Handbook is horrible, or wrong. It's good for what it was intended to do - teaching primary students the basics. The Handbook does give the average pilot some basic fundamentals to practice and think about, but nothing in the form of advanced techniques. What I'm saying is that it's somewhat suitable, but also grossly inadequate for advanced pilots like us when it comes to engine out training.

That said, it's time we took a much deeper dive into the specifics to training for the engine out emergency. Teaching advanced techniques is what this book is designed to do. We are now going to take it to the next level!

The Overhead Practice SFO for GA

Call it what you want; the overhead glide, the 360 degree power-off spiral, the Kobayashi Maru, etc. In this section, we are going to dive deep into what F-16 pilots call the Overhead SFO. Adapted from multiple GA sources, we will highlight how I believe we should all be training. With this overhead SFO, we will illustrate and describe how to accomplish an engine out pattern and landing in your GA single engine aircraft from a point above the landing surface.

Recall our earlier segment about the use of the Overhead SFO pattern for the F-16. The chief takeaway there was that it would be quite rare to be directly above the airfield and then lose the engine. While certainly possible, this scenario is not very probable. It is, however, possible that you could lose your engine and glide to a position *above* your chosen landing spot, in which case this overhead pattern and approach would be valid. That idea is a viable tactic.

My point is that you should use this overhead type of pattern for your initial engine out training, and decide later on how you will recover your aircraft in a real-world situation. You must decide when and if the overhead method will work for you, given the circumstances and your energy level for the day that your engine decides to stop playing.

Setup

Before we jump right into how we will execute the overhead engine out pattern, we need to decide on how to set it all up. Some consideration should be given to where you will do this training. For me, my tower controlled field is quite busy, and often the pattern is full of primary students and helicopter training as well. It can be done at my home field, but not always very well and with any consistency. I would also rather choose to focus on my engine out practice versus keeping my head on a swivel and deconflicting from other aircraft in the pattern.

For this reason, I have chosen a point out in the practice area as my reference "runway." I mentioned this reference point earlier during the flight test discussion, and it is the same point I have used for my training as well as the flight tests. My recommendation is that you find a location away from built-up areas and heavy populations, and away from GA flight training zones if possible. The point should also look like a runway or a field, and be easily identifiable from the air at some distance. A road or a field is fine; just make sure it is visible and clear, so you can get some consistency to your training.

If you have access to a sleepy, uncontrolled airfield, this also works, and may be the best choice for your training so long as you can ensure deconfliction from any other air traffic visually and on the radio, should someone else choose to come in and land or takeoff.

At whatever point you choose, I recommend you get some solid position data on it. You will need to know the elevation of your point (the imaginary runway surface) and if possible you might consider locating its GPS position too. I don't always use the GPS distance to my reference imaginary runway. However during the initial stages of your training (and later when we cover IMC engine loss), you might benefit from dialing up some kind of reference in your GPS that can give you range to the point. Later, as you get better with your practice, you will be able to pick a point anywhere on the earth and execute a nice glide to it, regardless of your GPS settings.

When it comes to GPS reference points, also be cognizant of whether or not you are using "brick one" for your point and reference numbers, or the center of the airfield. When you call up a pre-loaded airfield in your GPS library, usually it defaults to the center of the field. Realize that the center of the field and the start of the runway landing surface, or "brick one" can sometimes be 0.5 nm or greater different. That alone will make some of your practice glide numbers look drastically off.

You will also want to be gentle with your engine during this training, as gentle as you can be. We already mentioned some gliding pitch and power settings for various types of GA singles. If you are training in something with fixed gear, you might be faced with having to do these maneuvers with the power at idle. Sorry, your engine might cool down some during your practice, so keep an eye on that when practicing.

If you are flying a retractable gear aircraft, I would recommend that you make a note on your kneeboard card (or whatever paper documents you fly with) as to your two chosen configuration and power settings so you can reference them if needed during the simulated engine out. For most Bonanzas, setting number one (#1) will be about 12-15" MP, Prop 2,500 RPM, gear down, flaps 10 degrees, and tweak the power for 1,000 fpm VV. Setting two (#2) is all the above, but with power at idle.

Additionally, you might want to consider a minimum altitude for your practice. How low do you want to go and execute a recovery? Depending on your aircraft and your currency, you will have to make quite a few configuration and power changes to execute the go around, so adding a bit of altitude pad (especially early in your training) would be wise. I would recommend you always calculate a minimum altitude for your training and adhere to that altitude during the execution portion of your simulated emergency patterns.

The last part of the setup phase is to consider the winds. I like to get an idea of what the winds are doing at my practice point by looking at the weather at nearby airfield before I launch. I also have the benefit of a wind depiction and readout in my cockpit. This will give current live winds as I execute my practice patterns. Additionally, I would also look for some of the basic clues that we all learned about during our initial training about ways in which to figure out the winds on the surface. Seeing wind effects on lakes, smoke, and dust, and which way the cows are all facing are just a few examples. Keep those skills sharp and always look for ways to identify what the wind "down there" is doing. That alone can be a huge game changer with regard to your touchdown ground speed during a real crisis. Think about that.

Practicing the B-CAPs

As you begin to go out and fly some of this practice glide stuff, you will need to decide when and how you will begin the training profile. If you are flying with a CFI, you might want to pre-brief with him/her what you would like to do and when you would like to do it. You can also do all of this training solo as well, there are no restrictions to doing so.

What I recommend and normally do is to first decide that I am "engine out." With a CFI, you can have them surprise you and say "engine out" while pulling the throttle to your prede-termined MP. Either way, you must start the simulation some-where. From there I like to do the B-CAPs immediately. This serves to reinforce my initial actions given an engine failure. You can practice this a few times until you get good at just the B-CAPs. In my training, I do not actually execute the B-CAPs to their fullest, but instead I touch each lever or switch, in the correct order while reciting the B-CAPs verbally. You can also practice the B-CAPs on the ground, engine off if you want. As a reminder from the previous chapter, our new B-CAPs are as follows:

1. Glide - ESTABLISH
2. Fuel Selector - SELECT OTHER TANK
3. Aux fuel pump - ON
4. Mixture - SWEEP
5. Magnetos - VISUALLY CHECK BOTH

If no restart:
6. Aux Fuel Pump - OFF
7. Mixture - RICH
8. Magnetos - CHECK LEFT, RIGHT, BOTH
9. Alternate Air T-handle - PULL AND RELEASE

In the air however, I will set glide airspeed and sometimes even switch tanks, but I usually do not sweep the mixture or run the boost pump. Don't forget to trim for that best glide speed too. After the B-CAPs are done, pretend that the engine is not restarting and you will need to execute the "if no restart" B-CAPs (or non-CAP CAPS) as we mentioned in the previous chapter.

Once those are accomplished it is time to get the aircraft configured for your glide profile. As mentioned earlier, if you are a fixed gear kind of plane, there might not be much you can do besides pulling the power to idle. If you are in a retractable gear single, then park your airplane in your known #1 glide configuration. For Bonanzas, this is where you set your ABS numbers and tweak the throttle for about 900 - 1,000 fpm VV.

Lastly, don't forget your Securing the Engine checklist steps and be prepared to *simulate* turning the fuel selector to off, mixture to cutoff, and magnetos off (but please don't actually do any of these during your training!) Think about when you'd drop the gear and any flaps, and when lastly you might switch off the electrical system.

There will be a lot of switch touching and simulations going on at this point, again, don't actually do any steps, but be thinking about them and touching the appropriate levers and knobs. Following that practice setup and B-CAPs, your goal now is to fly the plane and practice your energy management.

SFO Overhead Pattern Description

The standard overhead SFO pattern consists of three important points in space. These are called "Key" positions and can be thought of as windows or checkpoints in the air that you are trying to fly through. These are what Mr. MacDougall referred to as "energy targets" in his above passage.

The point directly above the landing point or target is called High Key. High Key altitude is set, and based on your particular aircraft's glide ratio. Typical High Key altitude for most GA single engine aircraft is about 1,500 feet AGL (typically three times your 180 degree power off glide altitude lost). You should be aligned with the runway, or chosen landing surface, pointing into the prevailing wind at High Key.

Low Key is the next typical window, and is a bit more nebulous of a point. For us, Low Key is typically abeam the touchdown point and 1,000 feet AGL pointed 180 degrees the opposite direction from the starting heading and runway heading. Remember that technically Low Key (while often depicted as a hard number and position in space) can and usually will be an imprecise point that the pilot can adjust based on energy, winds, and spacing for that particular glide profile. It's okay to adjust your Low Key position to make the SFO pattern "work." For training and practice, however, you should attempt to hit that set window of 1,000 feet AGL abeam the landing target point, but adjustments to that window are also permissible with gained experience.

Base Key is typically the final checkpoint. Located about like a normal Base position in a normal pattern as far as offset and distance goes, but instead the Base Key checkpoint is typically double the normal pattern's Base altitude at this location. Base Key is 90 degrees heading differential from the landing surface or runway, and about 500 feet AGL.

Historically, there have been a number of different methods from a number of different sources on how to execute an overhead practice glide. And none of them look or smell much like the above brief description. One such example is the American Bonanza Society's recommendation found in figure 23. Note the 2,500 AGL high key, 1,500 AGL "Downwind Key" the 1,000 AGL Base Key, and something called a Straight-in Key.

ABS Overhead SFO
Figure 23

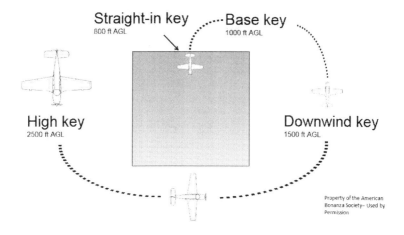

Property of the American Bonanza Society– Used by Permission

While these numbers are certainly doable, they are ultra conservative, and steep. Recall from our gliding turn tests that an average glide in the Bonanza will cost you just 500 feet of altitude in a 180 degree turn. The ABS Key numbers have you losing 1,000 feet in the first half of the maneuver and 1,500 feet in the last half of the maneuver. These are achievable, but are very high for every Key position.

The ABS numbers are for a dirty airplane with a windmilling propeller, basically our aforementioned worst case scenario.

The knowledgeable folks at the American Bonanza Society state that they purposely train pilots to fly high on this style of approach. They do this to allow for an altitude "pad" and to help pilots not get low and come up short on the landing surface. This technique also allows for the landing gear to be lowered in a Bonanza which significantly increases the sink rate. "If we teach pilots to "aim high" in their glide and they successfully repeat that performance in a real-world engine failure, they'll be in a position to extend the landing gear on final and still make their field" (T. Turner, personal communication, May 2016).

This technique does have some merit. They are indeed keeping you above the wire with this style of approach. However, how much pad is too much, and how much extra altitude will cause a landing surface overrun? Additionally, how confident are you that you can increase your descent correctly with the added drag of the landing gear? Obviously, it will take some practice. I prefer to have some known descent angles and sink rates, and practice to those sight pictures vice a random "space shuttle" style approach where you just stay high.

The ABS guys also recommend here our previously detailed engine and power settings, and 700 – 900 fpm descent rate to obtain the magical best glide replication. These pitch and power settings do indeed work, and will increase the longevity and happiness of your engine, but we also know that 900-1,000 fpm will be a more realistic baseline glide VV. I recommend that vertical velocity when training.

The earlier mentioned FAA Airplane Flying Handbook also contains depictions of the similar 180 and 360 degree power off approaches. While the Handbook's illustration and coverage of the maneuvers are not very consistent or accurate, the altitudes it recommends for our typical GA single are surprisingly close to the next example we'll look at, the T-34 dash 1.

The T-34 is a military Bonanza, used for many years as a primary trainer for the USAF and the US Navy. Because it was a military trainer, we also have the benefit of the old T-34 military manuals for guidance. The T-34 has an identical wing, landing gear, engine, and similar weight to the modern Bonanza, so it stands to reason that the way in which the military guys practiced and trained would be viable today, and an excellent place to start for our engine out training. Let's reference the US Navy's T-34B NATOPS manual for their excellent depiction of the overhead SFO maneuver in figure 24.

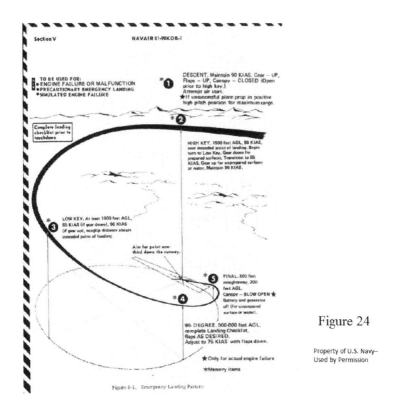

Figure 24

The T-34 manual shows a nice spiral wire, and an almost perfect circle ground track. This is optimum as it is important to stay "tight" to the runway. Fading too far away is a good way to get yourself low on energy and below the wire. More on this in a minute. I would recommend this type of pattern and abandon any ideas of a box or rectangular pattern for your SFO and engine out practice.

As far as altitudes go, the T-34 manual is exact. With a 1,500 foot AGL High Key and a 1,000 foot AGL Low Key after exactly 180 degrees of turn. That sounds a lot like our practice turn numbers in your average glide, huh? The second half of the maneuver gets a bit steeper after passing Low Key. Note that it has us losing 1,000 feet now for the remaining 180 degrees of turn. This is due to the landing gear being extended and the resultant drag and steepening of the glide. It will be up to you in the real aircraft to decide when and where to put down your landing gear and transition to that number two, worst case glide profile.

Other T-34 highlights from the manual include aiming for the first third of the runway as an initial aimpoint and the Low Key "window" of 1,000 feet AGL and abeam the landing spot. Perfect.

It also illustrates being abeam the landing spot with "wingtip distance." For me, in the Bonanza if I hold a perfect 30 degree bank turn all the way around, the wingtip will be somewhere below the landing aimpoint at Low Key. It is close, but not exact. This "wingtip distance" reference is approximate. The sight-picture you have here will vary for every pilot with different seating heights and of course different wings (i.e. different aircraft). A short wing Piper will look a lot different here from a long wing Mooney. Some practice as to what works for you will be important at this point, however generally speaking, putting the tip of the wingtip near the landing spot will be a close approximation of excellent pattern SFO runway spacing. We'll look into this a little deeper in a minute.

I want to be clear on this next point. With all the different techniques and options that the GA world presents the average pilot on the engine out glide, it can be quite confusing. Which one is correct or *right* for you? There are literally multitudes of differing guidance and examples of how to conduct and execute an overhead practice glide approach. You need to pick the one that works for you, and practice it.

However, I would also like to suggest the pattern and style that I believe is the most accurate, safest, and provides the best realism to train with. That profile is….

GA Overhead Engine Out Maneuver

I recommend the T-34 style of overhead SFO as your primary overhead SFO maneuver. This is not because it's a military-like maneuver, nor because it just so happens that this style of SFO is very close to the F-16 SFO and how we execute it in the Viper. I am recommending this style of overhead SFO because the numbers, spacing and altitudes are all accurate, and additionally this pattern is simple, while also providing you the best training on energy management techniques and sight picture development. Ultimately, this visual sight picture is what you are training for and developing and the T-34 overhead SFO does that the best.

There are actually some significant differences from the F-16 overhead SFO and the T-34 engine out overhead maneuver. The altitudes of course are grossly different, but primarily, the main real difference from the F-16 SFO and the T-34 SFO is that the F-16 SFO allows for a wing's level glide on "downwind" heading toward Low Key. This segment is quite short, but allows for an adjustment to the Low Key position and shapes the F-16 ground track more like an oval, not a circle like the T-34 ground track.

Remember that technically speaking, this whole overhead maneuver is heavily dependent on winds, turn radii, drag configuration, etc. The idea is to have a consistent plan and sight picture for training, but in the actual execution of this maneuver, the numbers and ground track might be slightly different. And they should be! Remember that doing whatever it takes to get the plane safely on the ground is what's important, not how well you hit each Key window.

Even in practice with the above T-34 pattern I am recommending, it's acceptable to float out your Low Key position by extending away from the landing spot to help nibble your way down to the wire and lose a little bit more energy, if needed. Just don't extend too far. You will however, by design, be high on energy at Low Key. With some practice, you will be able to see the sight picture and get a feel for the look angles and roll out of Low Key at the right moment headed for Base Key and do it perfectly. We'll look a little bit deeper into that technique shortly.

Overhead SFO Execution

Step-by-step, how do we execute this training maneuver? Here is what I do and what I recommend.

Start by approaching your High Key position at 1,500 feet AGL. You will be using visual references, but feel free to back yourself up with your GPS data as well. I usually approach High Key in a gentle left-hand bank, so I can see the point and prepare for my overhead.

Somewhere nearing High Key, the point and your makeshift (or real) runway will disappear beneath your nose. Do the best you can to roll wings level and track down extended centerline, while maintaining altitude and situational awareness as to where the first third of the runway and reference point are. Ideally, you'd like to be directly over the reference point (the landing aimpoint) when you "kill the engine" and roll into 30 degrees of bank to start the maneuver. Note your winds at altitude (if your avionics support this) and mentally apply them to your pattern. Try to visualize if the winds will be pushing you closer or farther from the runway as you execute the maneuver.

You will also see 0.0 nm on your GPS when directly above the landing reference point.

I usually recommend that you set up your aircraft for the glide while approaching High Key. For us Bonanzas and retract folks, reduce MP, lower the gear, set flaps to 10 degrees and trim for best glide airspeed. Keep tracking toward High Key in level flight. If you are practicing in a fixed-gear single, configure per your known best glide settings (which might be clean, and no real changes to drag devices) and be ready to cut the power to idle.

Upon reaching High Key, begin your execution. All you should have to do in the Bonanza at this point is reduce power to your known MP setting for best glide replication. If you are in a fixed gear single, you can probably pull your power to idle. Do that and then roll into 30 degrees of bank in either direction, it's good to practice both directions.

I'd also like to mention something about the B-CAPs. Some guys like to do all of the above and also practice the B-CAPs while executing the SFO. I don't recommend that for the following reasons.

One: There is a lot going on right at this point, you will be busy. Two: You are at (or nearing) High Key. Again, your engine will not fail right at High Key, so you are exercising this for no reason and probably should have done the B-CAPs much earlier. Three: The overhead SFO is designed for practice. Practice energy management and sight picture development. Work on those things now, head and eyeballs outside the aircraft please! There are actually a lot of good reasons to do it either way. That is, B-CAPs at High Key, or not at all. Early on in your training I recommend that we just focus on SFO setup mechanics, good entry parameters, and then just do the spiral and practice. If you want to recite the B-CAPs and touch each control lever, that's okay and it's an added bonus, but I'd honestly recommend practicing that elsewhere or well prior to High Key. For me, the overhead SFO is merely glide practice and sight picture development, I can practice the B-CAPs anytime.

Back to the execution phase. As you begin your turn, try to get a feel for the 30 degrees of bank and the nose low sight picture. Keep tabs on your airspeed and trim for best glide airspeed per your weight calculations. Understand that you would be gear up at this point if flying a retractable aircraft as well. If you are familiar with an instrument scan like during IMC flight, you will now have a new scan. I call it the SFO scan. The SFO scan is *airspeed, touchdown point, altitude; airspeed, touchdown point, altitude.* You should continue this song-and-tune repeatedly, as you continue all the way around the pattern. Got it?

Once you hit the first real checkpoint or window at Low Key, a lot happens. It's now time to *assess.* Low Key is the first true look that you get into how you are performing in this maneuver. It is your first chance to see what your aircraft is doing. You must assess how your glide is progressing and begin to decide on how to make any adjustments for portions that are grossly "off." Also, don't forget, that by design, you will be a touch high on energy here at Low Key.

If you are using a GPS point, you will see approximately 0.5 – 0.6 nm spacing for a well flown Low Key position. If you do the math for Low Key, being 0.6 nm away from the point (3,640 feet) and 1,000 feet high equates to a 15 degree angle or wire. About half of your recommended bank angle. That should offer an easy way to measure your Low Key performance too. For you low wing pilots, if the landing target is approximately halfway between the wingtip and the horizon (while you are in 30 degrees of bank), you should be in a perfect Low Key spot.

My other technique of briefly rolling out wings level at Low Key (discussed more in a minute) places the wingtip above the landing aimpoint. Coincidentally, the runway or landing surface will align slightly below, but close to my six degree wire wingtip mark (as seen in figure 17) for proper spacing, with the wings level. Technically, as stated, the landing point target should be 15 degrees below the horizon for a properly flown Low Key, so you can also use your "Rock & Roll" Hand Method for a quick performance check as well.

You high wing guys will have a much more difficult problem here at Low Key, as your wing will tend to visually mask or obscure the runway and landing environment. Lifting your wing and "taking a peek" at the touchdown point will be required to assess performance, however watch out for getting wide and subsequently low on energy as you roll out of bank.

At Low Key, I like to note where my wingtip is relative to the landing spot. I'll roll wings level for a second and "take a peek" and assess my spacing. This wings level "spacing check" is not mandatory, but is a good way to visually assess that sight picture and see how the pattern is shaping up. Remember, about 0.5-0.6 nm on the GPS is good spacing, and the landing point will be about 15 degrees below the horizon. Don't forget to check "Rock & Roll" with your hand if you can. I'll also look at my altitude on the altimeter, and as well as visually by looking outside. You need to be able to assess at this point how high above the ground you are, and if you are high or low relative to the wire. Again, the wire at this point in the maneuver is more of a gut feel, but your altimeter can give you a clue to your performance. You should see something close to 1,000 feet AGL.

So if you haven't caught on yet here, I'll echo the above crucial thought about Low Key and what it really means… energy assessment. Low Key is the window to assess your energy state and wire and start to make adjustments or changes to affect a proper touchdown. Good energy assessment at Low Key will allow you a valuable prediction of how the remainder of the maneuver will go.

Two other important things or items happen at Low Key. After my assessment, I will typically roll wings level and drive for just a few seconds. I call it the roll out maneuver. The length of this action takes time and skill to develop, but it is designed as an energy *depleting* maneuver. It's another way to take a nibble out of your energy. Remember here that you are also transitioning from a best or average glide profile to the steeper worst case glide profile, and you will by default, be high on energy. Part of that transition also encompasses putting the gear down, which leads me to my second important Low Key item...lowering the gear. Low Key is where we transition to that steeper worst case glide profile.

I lower the gear at Low Key (if they are not already down for some reason) and recall that for us, in training they are actually already down. So yes, here at Low Key I transition to my #2 glide profile and reduce power to idle. Note that the T-34 SFO depiction does not portray any kind of roll out maneuver; it is not mandated. However remember, Low Key is that nebulous point in space that you can adjust as needed to affect the perfect final 180 degrees of turn and touchdown. Either way, it is perfectly acceptable to assess your Low Key altitude while still in 30 degrees of bank and simply reduce power to idle when you see fit to begin your steeper glide. If the winds are stronger and down the runway, or pushing you away from the runway at Low Key, the roll out maneuver may not be smart, but the roll out maneuver does help you assess if the touchdown point is 15 degrees below the horizon or not, you're just using your wingtip as a guide.

Also, depending on your energy state, winds, and how far away from the runway you have flown during the first half of your SFO, you need to do that critical energy assessment and make a decision on how to continue. If you assess that you are low on energy, it is entirely possible that you might need to keep the simulated gear up and make an even stronger bid toward the runway.

For you fixed-gear guys, this may in-fact be all you can do. You might already be in the draggiest configuration that you can get, and you might be losing altitude and energy very rapidly.

My point is that your biggest chore at Low Key is to assess energy and either delay the turn to Base Key (if you are high on energy) and nibble your way down to the wire, or assess that you are low or below the wire (if low on energy) and make an immediate turn for Base Key or the runway.

As you depart Low Key, you should now be back in your 30 degree bank, checking airspeed and referencing the landing point. *"Airspeed, touchdown point, altitude; airspeed, touchdown point, altitude."* Things will get a bit steeper as you approach Base Key, and you may even start to sense some ground rush. You are looking for about 500 feet AGL at Base Key if the math and your new steeper glide are working out. If it is not working out, for instance, and you find yourself high or low at Base Key, you still have a little time to correct these energy errors.

If you find yourself low on energy here, about all you can do is continue the bid toward the runway, get that turn done quickly and start making ground heading toward the landing spot. Resist the temptation to stretch the glide and get slow.

Conversely, if you are high on energy the best option is to extend more drag devices (if you have them), shallow the turn toward the landing spot and in doing so lengthen the time it takes to get there and hopefully lose a little more altitude (making that ribbon longer). Lastly, if you are high on energy, you can consider a slip to reduce energy as well. Check your POH for slip limitations and do not exceed them, or you might be finishing this practice SFO for real!

Note that you have far more options to fix a high energy situation than a low energy situation. That is why it's important to stay on or above that wire and take those small bites out of your energy to slowly work your way down to the wire. Going below the wire presents you with limited options and is a most certain path to landing short.

The Base Key position is your final checkpoint. You should see about 500 feet AGL if the numbers are working out, but more importantly you should be starting to really notice the ground coming up as well as other visual cues. You should also be running your SFO scan and ensuring you are not too slow or fast. The most important part of the Base Key position is to assess LOS for your touchdown point. With a little practice, you will be able to quickly determine if you are high on energy or low on energy by examining LOS of the landing surface, and make the appropriate corrections to your wire. You only have about 30 seconds left until touchdown, now is the time to fix the last part of your wire and nail that new aimpoint at brick one. Transition your first third aimpoint reference to the beginning of the runway and look for the LOS rates of that point on the earth. Attempt to zero out the LOS for that new brick one point and "cash in" all your remaining energy now to arrive on that new wire and make that happen.

The final portion of this maneuver is of course the landing phase and touchdown, or the go around. More on these in a few minutes. From Base Key to the runway, there is not much left to do except attempt to touchdown at brick one, think about rolling flaps, and anticipate the flare as your vertical velocity will be pretty hefty at this point.

While we reference and publish numbers, altitudes, speeds, and wires for this Overhead SFO maneuver, the truth is that it's a visual maneuver, and you the pilot just need to *make it happen*. What I mean is that you can honestly fly any ground track, bank angle, and wire that you need to affect a perfect touchdown. Again, *that* is all that really matters. Now in reality, this all takes time and skill to develop. We need to start with some known checkpoints and fly to those points so we have some mental references and a baseline understanding. Try flying your first five to ten practice SFOs by the numbers, referencing the checkpoints and comparing your parameters, and see what you discover. After that, feel free to start to adjust your overhead SFO as required, and do some of that pilot stuff!

Lastly, should you find yourself in the heat of battle someday, with an actual engine out aircraft, and you can't recall any numbers or parameters, it should hopefully be fairly easy to remember one special location. That location is abeam the landing spot, on downwind and 1,000 feet AGL. It smells a lot like a downwind pattern, or Low Key huh? Regardless, it's a good reference to imbed in your memory. If you can get there, you should be able to make it to your landing spot.

Final Thoughts: GA Overhead Engine Out Maneuver

Wrapping up our discussion of the overhead SFO, there are a few final points I'd like you to think about and plan for in your training. The first point is thinking about when to lower landing gear (if you have them to put down or choose to based on terrain), and when to lower flaps. Recall that from our earlier lesson that it really depends on the situation you are faced with (your energy situation) and when and if you'll use either or not.

During the execution of the overhead SFO practice maneuver, much like the B-CAPs, I am NOT going to do much with my gear or flaps. I will configure like we stated with the ABS settings, but after that, for practice, I am done with configuration changes. It's good to think about these configuration changes as well as our securing the engine checklist steps, however, I will generally be focused on the maneuver, energy management, and sight picture development. I will not spend too much time messing with flaps and such. It's ultimately up to you, but remember, it's just training. When it comes to the real deal someday, you might have to lower the gear somewhere and accept that steeper sight picture, and roll flaps to full of short final if you elect to.

Also, consider the landing terrain from our earlier examples. If you choose to stay clean and keep the gear up, realize that generically, you would just then lose just another 500 feet of altitude in the turn from Low Key to Final. In this case, you'd simply end up 500 feet high over the threshold, and subsequently high on energy and dealing with a long landing. Be prepared for that. If for some reason you are keeping the gear up, you may need to widen the overhead SFO to avoid landing fast and long. Occasionally I even practice a clean glide SFO and keep the aircraft parked in glide profile #1, all the way around the profile.

Additionally, some consideration should be given to *actually* touching down on the runway during training. It goes without saying that if you are practicing over a field or a road as your chosen landing surface that you should not touch down, especially if you are going to jeopardize safety or violate any FAA object clearance limitations. If you are training over an actual runway, and have clearance to land, at some point in your training you might consider an actual SFO to a flare and touchdown. I typically fly my practice SFOs to a low approach, but it might be worth practicing to an actual touchdown as well.

I would only recommend doing this after you have attained a fair bit of practice engine out experience, and even then I'd only do them with a safety pilot or CFI aboard. There is a lot going on in the landing phase, a steep approach, and some unusual power settings and speeds. Think it through, plan it out... and fly safe.

GA Straight-In Pattern Description

The straight-in SFO pattern is an entirely different approach to engine out training. While not a very difficult pattern to execute in practice and theory, there are some interesting and complex points to consider while training with it. Familiarity with this type of approach is a valuable tool for any pilot's bag of tactics.

I also realize that this type of engine out approach is not taught to General Aviation pilots and CFIs, but I do believe it has merit for a number of reasons, and not just because the USAF teaches it. The primary reason I feel this approach is important to train to is that it is realistic. What I mean is that more often than not, in my training and flying, a viable recovery landing field or road seems to be farther away and not directly under or near my aircraft. I feel that if I was to need to execute an engine out glide that my preferred landing site will be one that I will need to fly to, and I will have to drive relatively straight there to make it and execute my landing. Having a viable landing surface at some distance seems often more likely than having a landing spot directly under my aircraft. Most of my local flying also entails departing over heavily urbanized areas, and all possible engine out landing sites are quite far off and away, outside of the heavily built-up cityscape below me. Reaching a landing spot outside of town is a major concern.

Secondly, the other reason that this method is important to you is that it is a slightly more math-heavy style of approach, and it teaches something called line-of-sight (LOS). Flying the straight-in SFO will require you to crunch some numbers, and that alone is good practice for understanding the three dimensional relationships of energy and sight pictures. That significant reason also has a key secondary training benefit… planning and executing the IMC engine out approach. We will deliberate the IMC engine out situation shortly, however parts of it will look quite similar to a regular straight-in engine out pattern we are about to discuss. The line-of-sight reinforcement is identical to your normal landings in that you are looking for the spot that isn't moving in your windscreen, the one with zero LOS. This LOS sight picture is the most important part of your straight-in SFO practice.

Lastly, one reason this type of pattern is valid is that it might be new to you! Go figure, right? I enjoy mixing up my training, and trying something new from time to time. I think you will too, and I also think that you will learn something from trying a flameout glide in this fashion.

The straight-in SFO like the overhead SFO *sort of* has Key positions, though in the F-16 world they are not called Keys. The F-16 dash-1 defines different "points" in space along the extended centerline from the runway that you can think of as different Key points if you want. When different energy states occur, at these different points, different things happen in your execution of the recovery.

Let's have a look at figure 25 for a sketch drawing of our straight-in SFO. This drawing is modified from the F-16 straight-in SFO diagram, but the numbers and parameters have been changed to fit us in our General Aviation single engine machines. Note that this drawing looks very similar to our earlier Baseline Glides chart seen in figure 21.

Straight-In SFO
Figure 25

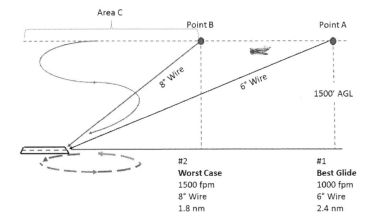

Initially, the straight-in engine out procedure looks a little complicated, but in reality it's fairly easy. Let's break it down and examine each of these Points and what is occurring at each one.

Before we start, note that each point corresponds to an altitude above the field. This altitude is a reference altitude and depicted as a horizontal line on the drawing above the ground and runway. Remember that you are on extended centerline for this maneuver and this reference line is above the runway and goes out along the extended centerline. For us in the Bonanza, and most GA singles, this line will be 1,500 feet AGL, as this is the basic minimum required altitude you would need to execute a 360 degree overhead approach.

Point A is therefore defined as a line from the runway threshold, at our *best glide* angle, all the way up to 1,500 AGL. If we do the math, Point A lays 2.4 nm from the threshold (no wind). You can also easily calculate that ratio farther out if you choose. At 3,000 feet AGL you would need 4.8 nm, and at 4,500 feet AGL 7.2 nm would work, but those numbers can get complicated. Breaking it down further, this wire is again, about 1.7 nm per 1,000 feet, and I'd ask that you commit Point A to memory as 1,500 AGL and 2.4 nm from the threshold.

Point B lies at our predicted *worst glide* angle (gear down, windmilling propeller) at 1.8 nm from the threshold. You can do the math there too and see that we need 3.6 nm at 3,000 feet and 5.4 nm at 4,500 feet AGL. This is also the same relationship for our 8 degree glide or about 1.2 nm per 1,000 feet of altitude AGL. All of these points are of course no-wind.

Area C is defined as anything closer to the runway than Point B, or 1.8 nm at 1,500 feet AGL. If you find yourself in Area C, your only option from extended centerline is to execute some kind of overhead engine out pattern as continuing straight-in would cause you to land long.

I'll highlight here that during the straight-in SFO, the math is helpful and worth considering and practicing, however the landing point or runway line-of-sight movement and picture development is what we are striving for. Let's look a little bit deeper on how to accomplish this pattern.

Straight - In SFO Execution

The straight-in engine out procedure is all about prediction, LOS, and some math and numbers too. You are attempting to align with the landing surface at great range, and then setting up your best glide to that surface. At some point you will need to determine what sort of glide angle and performance you are making to the field and assess your energy. This can be difficult. Sight pictures can help immensely here. However distinguishing between a six degree and an eight degree wire at range from the target landing spot can be very problematic. It's rare, but sometimes the landing surface can even disappear below the nose cowl of your aircraft. You will most likely need some kind of GPS reference distance to the landing surface as well, to make the straight-in SFO work, but it is not required.

I recommend that in your execution of the straight-in SFO pattern that you randomly set it up, at random points and azimuths from the makeshift runway as well as with random altitudes too. Set up the straight-in engine out approach in the same manner that you set up the overhead engine out pattern, by slowing down to near best glide speed, trimming, and configuring for whatever method you choose to simulate your best glide.

Since you don't have a High Key point, you can technically set and begin your best glide anytime you want after parking your aircraft in your best glide profile setting #1.

Once established in the glide, it's now time to turn toward the field or landing spot you have chosen and begin to assess your energy state. To assess your energy, you can do the math for your distance to the field and determine what wire you are on. However I will argue again that the LOS sight picture if far more valuable and realistic to your training when VMC. *It is important to realize in the straight-in SFO that you are not only running the math part of the maneuver at 1,500 feet AGL,* you may need to run the math when farther out and at higher altitudes to assess performance. My point is that the 1,500 foot AGL checkpoint is simply the *final* checkpoint in a series of math and LOS crosschecks during the straight-in SFO.

Back to the execution. Once you begin the maneuver, you will immediately need to assess your energy state. Energy assessment can be very difficult during this approach, and it must be done continuously. You will need to crunch some numbers to get an honest look at how you are performing. Depending on winds and what kind of descent gradient you get as well as cowl size and seating height, you might have grossly differing sight pictures on any given day. There are too many variables here to even list a rule-of-thumb, however the LOS rates of the runway are your primary "clue" to how you are performing. If we had a HUD and a FPM, it would be easy, but just looking out the window, it can be very challenging to honestly assess energy.

About the only way you can visually determine and assess how the glide is progressing (outside of the math and numbers method) is to assess the drift of the landing spot in your windshield. This, again, is called line-of-sight. Similar to a normal landing, you might have heard the saying before that "the point on the runway that isn't moving in the windscreen is where you will hit." Well, the same holds true here. See if you can find the point that doesn't move in the front windshield, or the point with zero line-of-sight movement. Ideally, you want that landing spot you are aiming for to be the point that isn't moving.

If the landing spot is drifting down in your field of view (closer to the cowl), you are gaining energy relative to it (and likely progressing toward a steeper wire, this is good!). If you are noticing the landing spot drifting upward in your windscreen, you can assess that you are losing energy and will most likely not make the field and land short.

If you are low on energy, you may need to turn directly to the field regardless of runway alignment. If you are high on energy, you should be able to turn away from the runway and glide toward the runway extended centerline in effort to align with the runway as well as lose a little bit of energy in the process. In that case, you are making your "ribbon" in the sky longer and subsequently losing energy to capture your wire.

The above is a typical glide profile when I practice the straight-in SFO. I will normally glide toward the field until I start to assess that I am between Point A and Point B (somewhere out at range and much higher than 1,500 feet AGL of course), then I will turn away from the runway and attempt to align with the extended centerline with my excess energy. Hopefully, I can make the extended centerline while remaining high on energy, but if not and I assess that I am low, or getting low and approaching that six wire, I will turn back toward the runway and accept my energy state and attempt to make it to the field. As I approach 1,500 feet AGL, I will do a final check of my range and assess where I am (hopefully) between Point A and Point B and then complete the maneuver to my minimum altitude and execute a go-around.

But back out during your glide, at range, if your glide is going well and you are gaining energy, you will start to feel *high* relative to the landing surface, and the runway will begin to get close or even disappear below the nose. As you approach this sight picture, there are two things you will need to prepare for (and possibly execute) to affect a nice touchdown on your spot.

The first is assessment of that one-to-one ratio we talked about. If you are approaching that one-to-one but not quite there, pilots of retractable gear aircraft can simply drop the gear and steepen the approach to landing. You are deliberately picking up your #2 glide profile (the dirty profile) in hopes to intercept Point B (at 1.8 nm) as you know your performance during this kind of approach. Once the gear are down (remember, for training, just set idle power here) the remainder of the new steep eight degree approach will be fairly simple to complete.

The second thing you can do is to again assess your energy with the one-to-one ratio. If you are at a true one-to-one (i.e. 1.5 nm to go at 1,500 feet AGL) or anywhere past it (closer to the runway) you can no longer drop the gear and land straight ahead. You are past Point B (or you will be once reaching 1,500 feet AGL) and already in Area C. Doing this might put you really long and an excursion off the departure end of the runway is a real possibility. What you need to do at this point is realize you are entering or have entered Area C, and it is now time for an overhead profile. Luckily, you are well trained and prepared for those!

At this point, if you enter Area C and you have retractable gear, *keep them up*! You now have a new energy problem to solve and a 360 degree gliding spiral approach to execute. Remember our best glide numbers and altitude lost? You will need to transition to that mentality and attempt to stay clean as long as possible. Knowing that it takes about 1,000 feet to do a 360 degree gliding turn (in a retract single), you should be okay on energy and altitude. However, you still need to glide toward and above the landing surface, which could eat into your available energy quickly as you fly toward a makeshift High Key position.

The best thing to do here is, again, stay clean, execute the gliding 360 degree pattern as practiced and anticipate being low at Low Key and Base Key. Plan for possibly either lowering the gear very late or not at all if it means making it to the planned touchdown spot. There will be a lot of energy management issues to deal with here and a temptation to overbank the 360 degree turn and speed up the pattern. That is a viable option, however one must be extremely careful not to get distracted and enter a stall.

Again, for training in the straight-in engine out pattern, it is helpful to have a way to measure distance to the landing surface, so you can start to see and learn the sight pictures for the day you may need to use them. As a bare minimum, you should know your Point A and Point B ranges at 1,500 feet AGL (2.4 and 1.8 nm respectively) and reference those during your simulated glide practice sessions. But I would also like you to focus on your landing spot LOS picture and begin to develop a feel for how that looks.

Go out and give it a try, it is really quite simple!

Final Thoughts: GA Straight-In SFO Maneuver

The straight-in SFO seems really simple, but there are a lot of things going on during the execution of it that can make it somewhat difficult. It is also much more of a "Zen" maneuver that will take you time in your specific aircraft to master. Without the aid of a HUD and a FPM, it can be extremely difficult to judge where in-fact the aircraft will touch down. Math and numbers can help a ton here, but again, there is no guarantee that you will have those ready and loaded into a GPS during an actual engine failure situation. This is why it is again critical for us GA guys without the technological benefits of HUDs and such to really develop those sight pictures and gain a sense for line-of-sight motion of the landing spot. Ultimately, that is what you are developing with the practice straight-in SFO.

Additionally, not knowing the elevation of the landing surface makes it really hard to accurately find Point A and Point B or predict where you will be when you cross that 1,500 AGL line. But I am confident, with a little practice on the straight-in SFO, you will begin to be able to visualize your relation to the two wires and effectively put the aircraft down safely right where you want it. Give it a try!

Landing Site Selection

There is a thread on BeechTalk (the online quintessential Beechcraft forum) that was developing about the same time as I was finishing this book. It was covering the safest way to crash land an airplane. This thread was over four pages and had over 60 replies already at the time of this writing.

Reading through all of its pages and all the various comments by multiple pilots and self-proclaimed experts, one thing became really clear to me. That is, there are a tremendous amount of variables when it comes to landing site selection and the engine out situation, and picking the best landing site and aircraft configuration for that pending crash can have a multitude of outcomes.

A common theme did emerge however after reading the lengthy postings, aside from the sheer number of variables involved. That key theme was that slower airspeed, and the rate of deceleration as well as a shallow angle of impact seemed to be something that all could agree upon as being the most survivable. The slow and shallow landings that some folks cited examples for all seemed to have mostly good results for the occupants of the stricken aircraft.

The other chief concern in the thread, and I would agree, is the concern for flipping the aircraft over during an unplanned emergency landing. While not entirely catastrophic to the occupants (sometimes), a post-crash aircraft flip would seem to increase the chances for fire, injury, and fatalities. Those with the ability to keep the gear retracted tended to want to do so, while there were also healthy examples of aircraft flipping over when the nose wheel "dug in" to the soft surface and caused a flip.

I do concur with these thoughts. One poster on the forum said something to the effect that if you are not willing to bet your life on the uncertainty of the actual state of the landing surface material (hard, soft, etc.), and you have retractable gear, then you should land gear up. I would tend to agree.

For me, if I can land engine out on a surface that I would consider taxiing or taking off from, then I will lower the gear and land on it gear down. If it's a soft surface or a field of heavy thick crops, or a desert full of scrub-brush, I wouldn't be taking off from those environments so my gear will stay up if forced to land there. That is my game plan, and I'm sticking to it.

Getting data from the accident reports on this sort of post-crash damage is difficult to gather. However the preponderance of the limited data I could find and associated pictures seemed to point to highway and road landings with gear down looking pretty survivable. Those landings in fields and deserts with the gear down had a much higher rate of nose damage, flips, ripped off nose gear, and crunched firewalls.

The 1958 T-34A dash 1 has a warning in its emergency procedures section as well. Remember that the T-34 is basically a tandem-seat Bonanza, with an identical wing and landing gear. This warning in the manual states: "Make no attempt to land on unprepared or unfamiliar terrain with the landing gear extended" (T-34A Flight Handbook, 1958). The more modern T-34B Navy flight manual also has a similar warning in its manual. That warning states: "When landing with the gear down on unprepared surfaces, the nose gear may collapse from contact with rough terrain and may cause the aircraft to invert making egress difficult. When the condition of the landing surface is in doubt, it is recommended that the landing gear remain in the up position" (T-34B Flight Manual, 1981). Of course flipping a T-34 and landing on its bubble canopy would be especially bad for the occupants, the idea still holds true for any aircraft in this situation, you want to avoid a flip. If you have the choice and the surface below you is unknown, I'd highly recommend you keep the gear up. If you have fixed gear, you need to land on the hardest and flattest surface you can find; your nose gear can also collapse in soft or uncertain terrain.

Here is another thing that I hear a lot of pilots say about the gear up or down decision when conducting a forced landing: "Having my gear down will absorb impact energy." I think logically, on the surface, this makes sense, and who wouldn't want to scrub off some impact forces by letting the landing gear take some of that brunt? This is a common sentiment, but the people who say that also may not have fully thought through what is happening in a forced landing and what the energy and impact forces are really like.

For example. In your modern car, what do the auto designers do to help make the car safer in a crash? They add seat belts and airbags of course. But what about the design of the car itself, the metal and structure? Have you heard of crumple zones? Sure, crumple zones are a means to slow down the massive deceleration forces that an occupant might feel in a car during an accident. If you look at the laws of physics, about the only way to lessen the impact G during a vehicle crash, is to stretch out the impact forces over *time*. Another way to look at it is to stretch out the impact forces over a large *distance*. Science has shown that vehicle impact forces and resultant G to the occupants of a car can, and are, survivable if those decelerating forces are 'smoothed out' over time and all the deceleration doesn't happen instantly.

A 2004 NATO study on human tolerance and crash survivability states, "It has been estimated that approximately 85 percent of all aircraft crashes are potentially survivable without serious injury for the occupants of these aircraft. This estimate is based upon the determination that 85 percent of all crashes met two basic criteria. First, the forces involved in the crash were within the limits of human tolerance without serious injury to abrupt acceleration. Second, the structure within the occupant's immediate environment remained substantially intact, providing a livable volume throughout the crash sequence" (Shanahan, 2004). In summary, this study is saying that most crashes are survivable if the aircraft structure remains intact, and the forces of the crash stay within our fragile human limits.

When it comes to shedding energy and deceleration effects on the occupants, the study also says this: "Rate of onset of acceleration refers to how rapidly the acceleration is applied. For a given magnitude and duration of acceleration, the greater the rate of onset, the less tolerable the acceleration"

(Shanahan, 2004). The author references a nifty chart as well that shows how the effects of a massive deceleration like 1370 G per second can in fact be survivable if spread out over time, or the length of that deceleration is prolonged by lengthening the onset rate.

A 2015 AVweb article titled *The Art of Crashing*, said this about aircraft crashes and deceleration:

> "How much of a difference will skidding, bouncing or dissipating energy over a distance make? A lot. An aircraft traveling at 60 knots coming to a full stop in one foot (as when hitting a cliff face head-on), will generate 160G. It is not a survivable crash. In fact, at that G-loading, bones will break and the human body becomes a liquid—it is not pretty.

> Spreading that same energy out over 10 feet drops the deceleration to 18G, which is bad, but survivable. Spreading the stopping distance to 30 feet takes you down to 5G, and if you can stretch the distance to 50 feet, where the deceleration is only 3G, you may have actually had worse turbulence than that" (Hart, 2015).

Let's take that "deceleration over time" concept one step further and apply it to our engine out aircraft. It is fairly obvious that landing, gear up, on any surface will allow the aircraft to "skid" along that surface and dissipate energy as it goes. That situation is desirable, of course. What isn't so obvious are the ways in which various parts on the aircraft will absorb energy when they meet a structure. As a pilot with an engine loss, what you don't know is how the landing surface is going to react to airframe bits like landing gear, propeller tips, wingtips and the like. It is quite possible that a protrusion such as the gear or a wingtip will impact an immovable object and produce a serious deceleration event. It's easy to say that the gear or some other part of the aircraft will help absorb energy as it rips off the crashing airplane, but how do you know that a wing impacting a tree for example won't rip off the wing or just cartwheel the aircraft instead? You don't. Just like you don't know if the landing gear will shear off the belly and scrub some energy and speed with it, or cause the entire aircraft to come to an abrupt halt, subjecting the occupants to massive deceleration forces.

Here is a situation you can compare all of this with. Think of driving your car on the highway. You're at 65 mph and you suddenly lose your brakes. Would you prefer to coast to a stop gradually if given enough road? Or would you prefer to hit something solid and stop quickly? I'm guessing you picked the former. Additionally, telling me that you will use the landing gear to scrub off some airspeed and impact forces in your air-craft is like saying you'll steer your now brake-less car toward a light pole to scrub off some speed. Your plan is to hit the light pole and it will slow you down. How do you know that you won't just stop instantly as you slam into the light pole? Or that the pole will break and absorb some of your energy and allow you to continue on at a slightly slower speed? You don't!

The same holds true for a crashing airplane. The ground is hard, those trees are firmly rooted. Predicting that pieces of metal airplane will shed off and slow you down during a crash is akin to aiming your car at a light pole and hoping that it will scrub off some energy during the impact. Personally, I want to be as *slippery* as possible and stretch that crash event out as long as physically possible.

I hope that we can put this argument to rest, and that you will adopt this philosophy if faced with a gear up or down decision in an engine loss situation. I'd like to think that the old military T-34 manuals and the laws of physics are on to something clever. If you're uncertain of the surface, leave the gear up.

The last thing I'll say about landing site selection goes back to an old saying, one that I know you've heard before. That saying is "altitude equals options." Pretty obvious of course, but it's true and something to remember. With altitude, you will have a much greater *choice* of available landing sites to choose from. Keep as much altitude as is safely possible during each phase of flight you are in and you will improve your overall survival chances greatly by simply providing yourself more available real-estate to choose from should your engine start to misbehave.

Steep Flares

I mentioned earlier a little bit of information about the actual flare and round out is needed when executing an engine out "steep" approach. Realize that an eight degree dirty approach is more than two times steeper and more than double the vertical velocity of your average every-day landing approach. You need to be prepared for this. The ground rush and "sinking feeling" that you get with this kind of approach can be eye-watering to the un-initiated.

For your first few attempts at any and all engine out profiles, I'd recommend a go around at your pre-briefed AGL altitude. Always do your go arounds with the proper methodology for your aircraft, but typically this chant sounds like *mixture, prop, throttle*. All forward, in that order.

As you get more comfortable and proficient, you can begin your go arounds at progressively lower (but safe) altitudes. Give yourself time to get accustomed to the aircraft configuration changes and the typical heavy nose-up pitch and subsequent trim adjustments that most aircraft require. You will also be doing all of that with a pretty significant downward velocity. Do not underestimate that. Once you have that vertical velocity under control and you are comfortable with it, you may be able to get your go arounds lower and lower.

As far as the actual steep flare goes, realize that somewhere above the flare point, you must begin a round out. You simply cannot drive a steep approach all the way down to normal flare altitude and flare and expect it to work out. I recommend that you start the round out about 100-200 feet above the touchdown surface. This altitude will vary depending on your skill and comfort level, as well as the aggressiveness of the nose-down descent profile you are flying. Bottom line: round out early to soften the very steep approach, and then enter the flare just like you normally would once you arrive on a normal looking approach and landing sight picture.

An advanced tactic here is to actually make your aim-point about 500 feet *short* of the threshold; as you know the round out will cause you to float a little and travel down the runway some amount before entering the normal flare.

Lastly, remember that in a real engine out scenario, you will be possibly rolling flaps to full here, so anticipate some float as you bleed off knots to your aircraft's normal touch-down speed. Every effort should be made to bleed off as much speed as possible while staying under control. The more speed you wipe off while airborne, the less you'll have to scrub off on the ground.

Overbanked Turns

I'd like to talk about one other important concept before we move on to our next subject. What I'd like to briefly review is the topic of overbanked and steep turns at low altitude. As you probably know, steep turns at low altitude are quite dangerous. The turns themselves are not inherently dangerous, but the stall / spins that can result from a steep turn and the close proximity of the ground, make the low altitude steep turn a hazardous undertaking.

Recall from your primary training days that a 45 degree bank turn requires 1.4 times the lift (1.4 Gs) for level flight, and the stall speed increase by 20%. A 60 degree bank turn requires twice the amount of lift (2 Gs) to retain level flight and the stall speed goes up 40%. For a mid-weight Bonanza at 3,000 pounds gross weight, and flaps up, stall speed is 61 KIAS. When that same aircraft banks up to 60 degrees AOB, the new stall speed becomes 86 KIAS, which isn't too far from our best glide speed we are attempting to fly. Extreme care must be taken anytime we are low and slow, but this becomes especially relevant when conducting a heavy task loaded engine out profile conducting turns low to the ground.

A typical pilot error during a real engine out scenario or training scenario is that a pilot finds himself / herself over-shooting final and low on energy. The mistake becomes a combination of stretching the glide (raising the nose, and getting slow) and attempting to "square the corner" and prevent an overshoot to align with the landing surface. Sometimes, even just an attempt to square the corner and overbank the airplane can place the aircraft dangerously close to stall speed and that critical angle of attack. Both of those control inputs might end up being the last ones the pilot ever makes. Low and slow is one thing, but low and slow and with *bank* angle is far worse.

Please consider your bank angle, and be very attentive to it when executing a practice or real glide down to the surface. Resist the temptation to overbank a turn to better align with your landing surface, and always fly your best glide airspeed. Do not get slow!

IMC ENGINE OUT SCENARIOS AND TRAINING

Anyone can do the job when things are going right.
In this business we play for keeps.

– Ernest K. Gann

One of the most significant engine loss situations you could ever face is losing the engine when IMC or above IMC. Being in or above the weather with an engine loss is a very serious situation and a very deadly situation as well. Staying upright, locating a suitable field to land on, and even getting to that field in an acceptable manner are made exponentially more difficult with the addition of "the soup."

There are however a few tactics that you can learn and use when it comes to engine loss in IMC. Most are pretty advanced, and all require some sort of way to measure your distance to the field. You will also, of course, need your current altitude and the field elevation. It goes without saying that surviving the engine out situation when in IMC takes a great deal of skill and possibly a greater deal of luck too. About the only way I know how to stack the odds more in your favor is to buy an ejection seat for your plane, or fly with higher weather minimums to give yourself time to glide through the weather and emerge below in VMC and make a successful recovery. That minimum altitude, as we said before, is up to you.

There are two methods for recovering after an engine loss in or above IMC; I call them the Spiral Over technique, and the Arc Technique. Let's break those down.

The Spiral Over Technique

One viable method looks and smells a lot like the Overhead SFO that you know and love so well. I call it the Spiral Over technique. The idea here is to get above an airfield, and ideally, if possible to get above the approach end of a runway at that airfield, and simply glide down in a spiral until you break out of the weather. From there, you hopefully can execute a successful recovery and touchdown. This method is basically what Mr. Anker did, and it worked out quite well for him. (He made it!)

As with all IMC engine out situations, you will need some kind of distance reference to the airfield in your avionics, and of course you will need to calculate and know your AGL altitude as well. Without one or the other, an IMC flameout approach is nearly impossible to execute with certainty.

There are no tried and true tactics for this method; however, there are a few things to think about when executing this approach. The first and biggest consideration is your glide angle or glide ratio. I'm assuming that you have accomplished any checklists and your B-CAPs, a restart attempt has been attempted and tossed aside and you are now committed to the engine out recovery. Once all that has happened, you will need to know which glide profile you are on and begin to do some calculations and math to affect the landing.

Are you gliding clean at your best glide (#1) style glide ratio, or are you draggy and gliding at the worst case (#2) style profile? Or something altogether different? You will need to understand those factors and how much altitude you are losing in each 360 spiral turn, and begin to calculate (if possible) how many turns you have until you reach the dirt. Remember, for our Bonanza folks, you'll lose about 1,000 feet for every best glide 360 orbit, and closer to 2,000 feet for every dirty *worst case* 360 degree spiral. Fixed gear pilots will be somewhere in between those figures.

My second consideration during this situation is where and when I'll break out of the weather, and what will I see when I do? You need to plan your orbit spiral appropriately. A turning spiral type flightpath directly over the center of the field may not be what you want to do. The reason being is that when you break out, you might be nearly over the center of the field, and executing a glide landing from a point above the center of the field at say 1,000 feet AGL could be difficult. You might not have enough runway available off the nose unless you are above a massive aerodrome like Chicago O'Hare airport or LAX.

If spiraling above the center of the field is all you can do, then that is okay. But if possible I recommend trying to spiral above the approach end of a runway. In this way once you break out of the weather you have the full length of the runway available for your use. The risk you take with this type of tactic is that you could emerge from the clouds pointed away from the field and possibly without ample altitude to complete the remaining turn back to the landing surface.

The final big consideration here (and we'll talk about this a bit more in the next technique) is where exactly is your reference point on the field that you have plugged in to the GPS? If you are on a perfect profile headed right to that point, remember you could be headed straight for the center of the field and that might not leave you enough room to land on the remaining runway if you pop out of the weather somewhere above midfield.

This technique is somewhat easy to execute, as it is relatively simple, provided you can actually get above an airfield. But this type of recovery can also have its "gotchas" and you will need to think about them and practice this type of pattern too.

The Arc Technique

The Arc technique is an engine out adaptation from a different jet aircraft I am familiar with as well as "bits and pieces" of the straight-in SFO VMC flame out pattern. The idea behind the Arc technique is that you are possibly farther from the recovery field, but also have enough energy to glide to an extended straight-in and execute a straight-in style recovery. Here's how it works.

With this method you find yourself some ways away from the landing field, engine out of course. You will of course need range, bearing and altitude to the landing surface as well as some kind of way to know the runway heading you are attempting to land on. I prefer to set up my HSI with the runway inbound course, so I have a depiction of that heading and my relation to centerline. Below is figure 26, which shows a basic sketch of the Arc technique.

IMC Arc Method
Figure 26

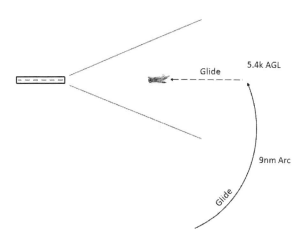

The plan in this technique is to get yourself into a position on, or near extended final with the appropriate energy to glide down the final approach course and land. What you need to do is first glide toward that extended runway centerline position and do some math.

We know that our best case glide has a glide wire of six degrees. This equates to about 600 feet for every nautical mile. If you were on a different glide wire, you could use that number as well. If you were on that worst case dirty wire, you would be at our previously mentioned eight degree wire and 800 feet per nautical mile now works.

But for our example, let's say we were gliding at our best case glide angle of a six degree wire. In this case, six becomes your reference number. Next, you must determine at what altitude you will reach the extended centerline at. Since that is difficult to predict, we simple need to fly a "DME Arc" toward that extended centerline and remain at the current distance from the field. In our example above we have found ourselves at 9 nm from the runway. All you need to do is multiply your DME arc by your reference number, and fly the arc. 9 x 6 equals 54, so I know that I will need to be 5,400 feet AGL when I reach extended centerline. It works for any DME you happen to be on. If you were on a 7 nm arc, well 7 x 6 equals 42, so 4,200 feet AGL works. A 15 DME arc (tougher math here) would necessitate a 9,000 AGL position on final. All you are doing is calculating the altitude you will need to have at centerline intercept, and flying an arc to that point to keep the math consistent and predictable.

Note in the diagram that we have a roughly 30 degree cone that extends away from the runway on either side of centerline. We'll call that The Cone of Justice! Flying in a glide and reaching your designated AGL altitude *exactly* on extended centerline final is very tough to do. Your goal should be to simply get within that rough 30 degree Cone of Justice, reach your designated AGL altitude and then turn towards the runway. It won't matter that you are a few degrees off runway heading; that's the least of your worries right? So fly toward the cone on your DME arc, run your math, and when you see your calculated number...turn in!

In reality you will probably want to lead that turn to final heading from the arc by about 250 feet, so 5,650 feet AGL for our 9 DME above example. But from there it should be quite simple, and you will merely need to point at the runway, cross check how your glide numbers are playing out and prepare to break out of the soup and hopefully see the runway within reachable distance off the nose.

The Arc technique is rather simple to do, provided you can do the math. The hard part of this approach is predicting if you can get into the Cone of Justice with anything close to your desired altitude. By quickly multiplying your reference number (most likely 6) by your distance to the field, you can see your energy state. If I'm at 8 nm from the field for example, and my reference number is 6 again, I come up with 4,800 feet AGL. If I find myself currently at or near 4,800 or so feet AGL, it's time to turn to the runway now! Otherwise, we can continue our glide toward the Cone of Justice at an 8 nm arc and patiently await 4,800 feet AGL.

The last important part of both this Arc method and the Spiral method as well, is that you need to remember that these "approaches" are emergency procedures. You have no guarantee of adequate terrain clearance, or clearance from obstacles. But you are also IMC with no engine, so *that* might be the bigger threat.

IMC Engine Out Practice

It is possible to practice these IMC engine out profiles. I would recommend that once you attain a fair bit of confidence and currency in the regular overhead engine out profile and the straight-in flameout as well, that you could begin to toss in a few IMC practice approaches too.

I would highly recommend doing these with a safety pilot, just like during your practice instrument approaches. You may want someone to help clear your flightpath as you will be heads down in the instruments as you practice and execute these IMC engine out procedures. With a safety pilot aboard, you can even put on the Foggles or a hood and see what you can do!

When I practice my IMC flameouts, I do them from some fairly "canned" setup parameters. What I mean by that is that I will script or plan my profile out in advance. For instance, I will go out to about a 9 or 10 DME position from my practice runway point, get about 6 to 7 thousand feet AGL and then set up my best glide profile #1 and fly my arc. I'll have the math pre-done and know what MSL altitude I will need to be at for my 5,400 AGL final centerline position too. It's all about the rehearsal and training.

These are still viable practice techniques, and I suggest that you try it this way on your first few attempts. Make it fairly scripted, and then go out and fly it as close to the plan as possible and see what happens, and what you can learn. You might be surprised. Much later, when you are a varsity expert on engine out practice, you can try a few simulated IMC recoveries from random positions and altitudes, and see what you can do, and what knowledge you can absorb.

Lastly, it's worth mentioning again that Synthetic Vision (SVT) is a good option for your engine out training and possibly real-world execution. If you have SVT and you rely on it, you might want to ensure it operates on battery power (when your engine quits) and also be trained up on its particulars. Be sure you use your SVT during your engine out training and practice so you can get familiar with it as well.

I would also like to close with one final reminder when it comes to IMC engine loss and practice for that scenario. Never forget about that old one-to-one ratio that was mentioned earlier. At least in the Bonanza, if you get close to that one nm per 1,000 AGL position, and you're in the soup…drop the gear, maybe push the prop forward, and ride that worst case glide down to hopefully a successful on airport landing.

Currency

Currency, or recency, is really the big sticking point when it comes to all of our engine out practice. Whether you chair fly these procedures or go out and fly them for real in your airplane, whether you focus on just the VMC stuff, or you practice heavy IMC style engine out recoveries, or all of it...it all boils down to *you and your currency*. In fact, that is really the root bedrock of this entire book. You may have some knowledge, and now you have more knowledge; but without practicing and training and using this knowledge, it will not amount to much when the engine quits.

I'll try not to get too preachy here, but what I want to get you thinking about is just how well practiced and proficient you are....or aren't!

How ready are you for that engine loss event? Are you comfortable with a basic understanding, or do you feel that you need to have practiced one or two glides every two to three weeks? For an individual, what amount (if any) is a good number of practice engine out events to be considered practiced and proficient?

The FAA mandates that we all do three takeoff and landings every 90 days to carry passengers. That is a currency to fly with others. They also ask us to do six approaches every six months to retain our instrument currency. Do you think we should have a currency requirement for practice engine out situations?

We sure did in the USAF and in the F-16 world. As already covered, we had to log 12 SFOs a year and we were considered out of currency if we went over 90 days without having done at least one practice SFO. We also had an ejection seat! Yet we still had a modestly strong currency for SFOs and practicing engine out patterns.

Interestingly, U-2 Dragon Lady pilots also carry an SFO currency of 45 days. In the T-6 Texan II, the USAF's foremost primary trainer aircraft, all of its instructor pilots are required to maintain a 60 day engine out practice currency. Even pilots of our newest fighter, the F-35, with its "new airplane smell" are required to do SFOs every 90 days.

The decision is yours. I will not mandate or even suggest a currency schedule here in this book for you to follow, however I think it does bear a little consideration and thought. I know the chances of engine loss are slim day-to-day, however remember, the outcome can be tragic to the untrained and unaware. I leave it up to you to decide how much you will practice engine out training.

You've taken the first step to developing your advanced engine out procedures and knowledge by picking up this book, now you need to complete the circle and go get some practical experience in your single engine aircraft of choice.

Post-Crash Tactics

Knowing what to do after the crash (hopefully just a bumpy landing) is an art form in itself. The intent of this book is to train and teach you on how to survive the *airborne* portion of an engine loss event, not the after-crash ground-based survival techniques.

Many volumes have been written about field survival, in every condition and environment known to man. There are literally countless books on the subject and even training courses that non-military personnel can attend. I am not a field survival expert by any means, however my USAF Survival Training and recurring training was adequate and exposed me to many practical techniques for surviving after an aircraft accident or ejection. Despite all of that, I will not presume to teach you how to survive in the field, and what actions you should take after egressing your crashed aircraft. I will however offer a few considerations that you might want to think about, and a few suggestions as well.

First, consider that you and your passengers will be hurt or physically impaired to some degree following an engine loss landing event. Hopefully you have shoulder harnesses installed in your plane. They alone increase your chances of survival tremendously. But either way, you should expect, and plan for, injury during an off-airport engine loss landing. Think about different ways to egress your aircraft, and any possible secondary egress methods like the baggage door, or emergency windows as in the case with all piston Beechcraft products. Knowing all the possible exits and ensuring your passengers know them as well, is an important consideration. Now think about egressing the aircraft when injured, and how that situation can become greatly complicated.

Secondly, how will you make contact with an outside agency or Search and Rescue forces? What are some methods for reaching them and communicating with them? A cell phone is the obvious choice, but chances are that it will be broken, or you will not have any cell service. You have an ELT that hopefully is signaling for you, but that only lasts so long as well. Please consider a few other methods for contacting rescue forces. Everything from simple flags and cloth visual signals, to smoke, flare guns and signaling mirrors, as well as GPS satellite phones are all great examples of signaling and communication methods. I prefer the ones that don't have batteries, are simple, and work quickly.

Lastly, I would recommend that you build your own survival kit, and store it in your plane. I am a firm believer that you should build your own kit versus just purchasing something "off-the-shelf" because in that way, you will know and understand what exactly you have. You can also tailor your survival kit to fit *your* needs and also construct it based on what terrain and environments you plan on flying over. A fishing kit might be useless over the desert southwest, but a small tube of sunscreen and a tarp for shade or water gathering might be essential. I'd also suggest some of the above mentioned signaling devices and some medical gear be added to your kit as well.

You should also consider whether or not you will just stash the survival kit in the back of the aircraft somewhere, or actually wear it. Yes, wear it. I know some GA pilots that wear a loaded survival vest on every flight. We wear them as well in the F-16, on every mission. Following a crash, there may not be time to return to a possibly burning aircraft to retrieve a survival pack. The decision is yours. Personally, I keep my kit in a soft sided nylon sling pack, and I keep it within arm's reach in my Bonanza's cockpit.

If you are looking for more information on post-crash actions and tips, please consider purchasing any one of the hundreds of survival field guides or books on the market that cover this subject. I am partial to the USAF Aircrew Survival Guide, or the USAF Survival Manual (AFR 64-4), both are a good place to start. You might also consider getting some formal training and even practicing some "camping" with just the items in your pack. Much like the CAPs or B-CAPs when flying, having a checklist or survival book in your hands after a crash may not do you much good. You'll need some practical experience in the field to increase your chances of being rescued in minimal time.

CONCLUSION

"Diligence is the mother of good luck."

– Benjamin Franklin

In the course of writing this book I read about multiple different, and interesting GA "crash" events that all occurred around the country, and while I was literally writing these pages. One event made the news when two teenagers crashed and sustained serious injuries in a Mooney on March 18, 2016 by running a tank dry. Later investigation found that they had good fuel in one tank, while the other tank was empty. Any guesses where the fuel selector was found? Spoiler alert, it was set to the empty tank.

There were also crashes of a V-Tail in Greenville, SC when a CFI and a student landed in a field for currently unknown engine problems, and a Cessna in Gainesville, FL on February 29th landed on a street. There were two souls on board in both of these incidents, and they all walked away. Coincidentally, the V-tail had its gear down for its landing on the grass field and nearly flipped over. Additionally, on 3 April there was a Lancair that landed on a San Diego freeway that ended up killing an occupant of a stopped vehicle on the side of the road. The passengers in the Lancair sustained life-threatening injuries. That exact Lancair also had a history of engine losses and has at least one other documented *previous* engine out event!

There were also many other crashes with fatalities, and some success stories as well. Too many to count and detail here. So why does it all matter? What is the chief take-away from all of it?

What struck me is the fact that these accidents keep on occurring. For whatever reason, these single engine aircraft crashed, and only time will tell on what the cause was. I applaud the surviving pilots for recovering and being able to walk away. But I think historical statistics are also going to tell us that about 70% of them will be pilot error related with a major chunk of that 70% being fuel mismanagement and fuel delivery related. I'm sure we'll also find in next year's Nall report that about 30% were also due to mechanical powerplant breakdowns.

The fact remains that these accidents do keep on happening, and a fair amount of them are engine related, and there will be more to come. Maybe I am just more cognizant of it now because that is the focus of this body of work, but the amount of crashed single engine GA aircraft seems to be steady, or even increasing. Despite the fact that we think we are all immune to an accident, we can all be confident that airplanes will continue to crash unfortunately.

I believe one of the primary methods we can mitigate that threat for ourselves, is to be prepared. Sure, proper maintenance and fueling and pilot in-cockpit procedures might protect us from calamity, however, we all need to be prepared and armed for the day when those barriers fail, and we are at the helm of our stricken ship looking over the cowl at a stopped propeller, and a quiet engine.

George Washington once said, "To be prepared for war is one of the most effective means of preserving peace." I happen to think he is right. I am not saying that by being prepared for an engine loss situation will prevent it from occurring altogether, however I do believe that by being prepared for that situation, that *war*, we will become better pilots and will in fact lower the chances that a future engine loss event will harm us. I think being prepared allows for a far better outcome should that unfortunate day come.

What are your thoughts on the engine out emergency? What were they before you read this book, and what are they now? You have had a chance to take your engine loss emergency knowledge to the next level, and hopefully I have shown you the path to becoming an advanced engine out pilot. Hopefully you have learned some of these tactics and may you never have to put them to real-world use.

Now is the time to begin your training with these new tools you have acquired. You have the knowledge, now you need the training. We have discussed a lot of different approaches to gaining that almighty experience that we all so desperately need in engine out situations. You now have the tools, but you need to develop the proficiency and skills to use those shiny new implements. In order to truly develop your advanced engine out skills, with all the tactics we've talked about, you need to go fly. It is up to you to actually go out there and do some of the stuff we have discussed. That practical experience of what we have covered is essential to your engine out survival.

Set aside some time on your next few sorties to go out and practice the maneuvers we have discussed, I think you will be pleasantly surprised how easy they really are, but also in what you will learn and take away from those flight experiences. I am confident that the lessons you learn, the sight pictures you develop, the pacing of cockpit tasks and the emergency procedures that you execute, in your airplane will make you a better and safer pilot.

Happy and safe flying.

SMART CARD

"It's not that I'm so smart, it's just that I stay with problems longer."

- Albert Einstein

N o one ever accused a fighter pilot of being smart. I'll agree to that. On any given day on any given F-16 mission, even in training, we have a wealth of information to recall and use to complete the sortie. From air-to-air tactics and logic decision trees, airspeed numbers, fuel and navigation computations, tanker track orbits and altitudes, air-to-ground weapons delivery parameters and explosive fragment clearance distances. It is a lot to remember, and often too much for one person to memorize quickly and recall inflight.

It isn't that we are all geniuses (although we sometime like to think we are), fighter pilots are just really good at organizing data. One of the ways we keep all the data consolidated is with something we call a Smart Pack, and inside of it were many things called Smart Cards. Detailed mission, weapons, and navigation data would be broken down on each Smart Card, and organized in the Smart Pack for easy reference during flight ops. The Smart Pack is basically a really good set of laminated crib notes.

Attached below is the *Engine Out Survival Tactics* Smart Card for your everyday use in your airplane. I've included some of the numbers and parameters from this book, and you should be able to print the card out and take it flying, or put a copy in your POH for quick reference. If the below copy is not suitable or printable, a downloadable copy is available on my website.

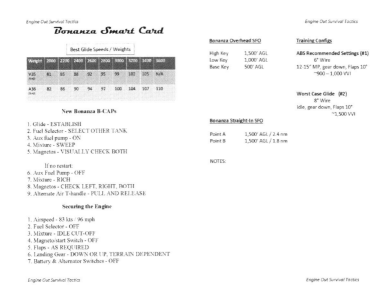

Engine Out Survival Tactics

Bonanza Smart Card

Best Glide Speeds / Weights

Weight	2000	2200	2400	2600	2800	3000	3200	3400	3600
V35 (KIAS)	81	85	88	92	95	99	102	105	N/A
A36 (KIAS)	82	86	90	94	97	100	104	107	110

New Bonanza B-CAPs

1. Glide - ESTABLISH
2. Fuel Selector - SELECT OTHER TANK
3. Aux fuel pump - ON
4. Mixture - SWEEP
5. Magnetos - VISUALLY CHECK BOTH

If no restart:
6. Aux Fuel Pump - OFF
7. Mixture - RICH
8. Magnetos - CHECK LEFT, RIGHT, BOTH
9. Alternate Air T-handle - PULL AND RELEASE

Securing the Engine

1. Airspeed - 83 kts / 96 mph
2. Fuel Selector - OFF
3. Mixture - IDLE CUT-OFF
4. Magneto/start Switch - OFF
5. Flaps - AS REQUIRED
6. Landing Gear - DOWN OR UP, TERRAIN DEPENDENT
7. Battery & Alternator Switches - OFF

Bonanza Overhead SFO

High Key	1,500' AGL
Low Key	1,000' AGL
Base Key	500' AGL

Bonanza Straight-In SFO

Point A	1,500' AGL / 2.4 nm
Point B	1,500' AGL / 1.8 nm

NOTES:

Training Configs

ABS Recommended Settings (#1)
6° Wire
12-15" MP, gear down, Flaps 10°
~900 – 1,000 VVI

Worst Case Glide (#2)
8° Wire
Idle, gear down, Flaps 10°
~1,500 VVI

Engine Out Survival Tactics

Engine Out Survival Tactics

Engine Out Survival Tactics

GLOSSARY / ABBREVIATIONS

ABS	American Bonanza Society
ADI	Attitude Direction Indicator
AGL	Above Ground Level
AoA	Angle of Attack
AOB	Angle of Bank
APS	Advanced Pilot Seminars
B-CAPs	Bonanza Critical Action Procedures
BFR	Biennial Flight Review
CAPS	Critical Action Procedures
CFI	Certified Flight Instructor
CFIT	Controlled Flight into Terrain
CG	Center of Gravity
CHT	Cylinder Head Temperature
DME	Distance Measuring Equipment ("distance")
EGT	Exhaust Gas Temperature
ELT	Emergency Locator Transmitter
EP	Emergency Procedure
FAA	Federal Aviation Administration
FBO	Fixed Based Operator
FPM	Feet per Minute / Flightpath Marker
FO	Flameout
GA	General Aviation
GPS	Global Positioning System

HUD	Heads Up Display
HSI	Horizontal Situation Indicator
ILS	Instrument Landing System
IMC	Instrument Meteorological Conditions
INS	Internal Navigation System
KGS	Knots Groundspeed
KIAS	Knots Indicated Airspeed
LAX	Los Angeles International Airport
L/D	Lift over Drag Ratio
LOS	Line of Sight
MP	Manifold Pressure
MSL	Mean Sea Level
MPH	Miles Per Hour
NATO	North Atlantic Treaty Organization
nm	Nautical Mile
NOTAMS	Notice to Airmen
NTSB	National Transportation Safety Board
POH	Pilot Operating Handbook
PTS	(FAA) Practical Test Standards
ROT	Rule of Thumb
RPM	Revolutions Per Minute
SFO	Simulated Flameout
sm	Statute Mile
SVT/SVS	Synthetic Vision
TAS	True Airspeed
T.O.	Technical Order

USAF	United States Air Force
Va	Maneuvering Airspeed
VFR	Visual Flight Rules
VVI/VV	Vertical Velocity Indicator / Vertical Velocity
Vx	Best Angle of Climb Airspeed
Vy	Best Rate of Climb Airspeed

REFERENCES

AOPA Air Safety Foundation. (2003). *2003 Nall Report, Accident Trends and Factors for 2002.*

AOPA Air Safety Institute. (2012). *23rd Joseph T. Nall Report, General Aviation Accidents in 2011.*

AOPA Air Safety Institute. (2013). *24th Joseph T. Nall Report, General Aviation Accidents in 2012.*

AOPA Air Safety Institute. (2014). *Air Safety Institute 2013-2014 GA Accident Scorecard*. Retrieved from http://www.aopa.org/-/media/Files/AOPA/Home/Pilot-Resources/Safety-and-Proficiency/Accident-Analysis/Nall-Report/2013-2014-Scorecard-V4.pdf

Busch, Mike. (2013). *Detonation and Pre-Ignition*. Retrieved from https://www.savvyanalysis.com/articles/detonation-and-pre-ignition

Deakin, J. (2016, June 4). Bonanza S35 in FL Today (8/23) – Fatal. Message posted to https://secure.beechtalk.com/forums/viewtopic.php?f=41&t=96330&start=15 (Membership req'd)

Federal Aviation Administration. (2004). *Airplane Flying Handbook FAA-H-8083-3A.*

FAA Advisory Circular AC 20-105B. (15 Jun 1998). *Reciprocating Engine Power-Loss Accident Prevention and Trend Monitoring.*

FAA Bulletin. (29 Apr 2005). *FAA Special Airworthiness Information Bulletin CE-05-51.*

FAA Fact Sheet. (30 Jul 2014). *Fact Sheet – General Aviation Safety.* Retrieved from http://www.faa.gov/news/fact_sheets/news_story.cfm?newsId=16774

FAA Safety. (nd) *Course 35, Use of Flaps.* Retrieved from *https://www.faasafety.gov/files/gslac/courses/content/35/376/Use%20of%20Flaps.pdf*

Flight Handbook T-34A, USAF Series. (10 Feb 1958). *T.O. 1T-34A-1*

Hart, M. (2015). *The Art of Crashing.* Retrieved from: http://www.avweb.com/news/features/The-Art-of-Crashing-223447-1.html

NATOPS Flight Manual. (2 Mar 1981). *Navy Model T-34B Aircraft.*

NTSB. (2013). General Aviation accident spreadsheet. Retrieved from http://www.ntsb.gov/investigations/data/Pages/AviationDataStats.aspx#

Price, J. M. & Groff, L. S. (2003). *Risk Factors for fatal general aviation accidents in degraded visual condition.* Retrieved from http://www.faa.gov/about/initiatives/maintenance_hf/library/documents/media/human_factors_maintenance/risk_factors_for_fatal_general_aviation_accidents_in_degraded_visual_conditions.pdf

Rogers, D. F. (1991) *Should You Turnback? Or The Possible 'Impossible' Turn.*

Schmelzer, B. (May 2012). *You were ready for this.* Retrieved from http://flighttraining.aopa.org/magazine/2012/May/feature-engine-out.html

Shanahan, D. F. (2004). *Human Tolerance and Crash Survivability.*

ACKNOWLEDGEMENTS

Amanda K. Champion, Author

Stephen E. "Gyro" Jaros, Fighter Pilot, Retired Airline Captain

Matt Anker, Bonanza Pilot

Jamie MacDougall, Bonanza Pilot

Joe Kirby, Cirrus Pilot

Tom Drew, Aviation Attorney

Brandon Ellsworth, CFI, CFII, MEI, Bonanza Pilot

James Gallagher, CFI, Bonanza Pilot, Photographer

Katy Gallagher, Editor

Brad "Crush" Wade, Bonanza Pilot, USAF Weapons Officer

David Jack Kenny, Air Safety Institute

Jeremy Chad "Jethro" Phillips, F-16 Instructor Pilot, USAF Weapons Officer

Scott "Fester" Fredrick, F-16 Instructor Pilot, Squadron Commander

Ed "KTOWN" Knouse, Test Pilot, Photo Chase Ship

The American Bonanza Society and Mr. Thomas Turner

Textron Beechcraft Aviation